KV-388-144

RUNNING TO WIN

Running to Win

IAN COFFEY

KINGSWAY PUBLICATIONS
EASTBOURNE

Copyright © Ian Coffey 1987

First published 1987

All rights reserved.
No part of this publication may be reproduced or
transmitted in any form or by any means, electronic
or mechanical, including photocopy, recording, or any
information storage and retrieval system, without
permission in writing from the publisher.

ISBN 0 86065 507 5

Unless otherwise indicated, biblical quotations are from
the New International Version, © New York International
Bible Society 1978.

Front cover photo: The Image Bank

Printed in Great Britain for
KINGSWAY PUBLICATIONS LTD
Lottbridge Drove, Eastbourne, E. Sussex BN23 6NT by
Richard Clay Ltd, Bungay, Suffolk
Typeset by Nuprint Ltd, Harpenden, Herts AL5 4SE

For Christopher, Stephen, Jonathan and Alistair—
four very special friends and the most important
congregation I ever have to face.

Contents

Foreword

The past few years have witnessed the sudden awareness of the importance of healthy diet and regular exercise in order to maintain our bodies at the peak of physical fitness. Our parks are full of early-morning joggers, and with the number of vitamin pills that some people consume it would not be a surprise to hear people rattling along to the office! The growth of the health food industry alongside the acute interest in the food-additive issue has served to strengthen the rising tide of interest in keeping fit and healthy to maximize our potential during our allotted time on the planet earth!

What a pity that as Christians we have been slow to follow the example—not to the extent of fanaticism, as in the case with some health 'freaks', but in our concern to maintain spiritual fitness. This is why I count it a privilege to have the opportunity of supporting and commending this latest work by my good friend and colleague Ian Coffey. Ian has a unique gift of being able to communicate biblical truth in a way that is relevant, interesting and applicable to our generation and, on reading this book—based on a collection of articles that have previously appeared in the pages of Buzz Magazine—I am sure you will understand my excitement and joy in being asked to write the foreword.

Ian draws from a wealth of experience in evangelism and teaching. He has served as a pastor in a local church and is now the Director of Evangelism for the Saltmine Trust—roles that have equipped him well for the communication of life-changing truth. I hope you find the book as refreshing and as helpful as I did and, if I may be allowed to extend the former analogy, I hope it will help you to fight the spiritual flab!

Dave Pope

Acknowledgements

It was a wet evening in November when Steve Goddard (then Editor of Buzz Magazine) finally tracked me down at a nightclub in Bournemouth. He telephoned to ask if I would consider writing a monthly column for Buzz Magazine, aimed at applying the message of the Bible to the issues that face us as Christians today. From that telephone call a happy partnership began and, though I found it very hard work, I began to enjoy the experience of writing what became known as the 'Coffey Break' column. I think I should add that the reason I was in the nightclub was because it had been taken over for a special evangelistic event!

I am grateful to Steve Goddard and all the Buzz team for their encouragement, ideas and patience—especially when it came to 'elastic' deadlines. In fact, they are the ones who first suggested that the monthly columns could be adapted to form this book.

Thanks are also due to Debbie Spicer, my personal assistant, who has undertaken the bulk of the work involved in putting this book together. She has spent hours adapting the columns, adding the 'Think through' sections together with the prayers and 'PS' comments.

As well as being a vital member of the Saltmine team, Debbie has become a special part of our family. She is also one of those Christians who has taught me much about spiritual growth.

I am grateful to Dave Pope, my friend and colleague in Saltmine, for writing the foreword to this book as well as giving so much positive input into my life.

Finally, I want to say thank you to Ruth, my wife, whose main ministry is keeping me in the ministry. Her commitment to the Lord Jesus and his kingdom leaves me standing. Being married to her is a rich experience of life, laughter and love.

Ian Coffey
Leicestershire
February 1987

How to Use this Book

The aim of this book is to provide practical Bible studies for Christian growth. It is designed to be used by an individual or a group meeting together for Bible study.

The thirty studies are grouped in sections covering either a Bible character, book or subject. The studies can either be followed in the order in which they appear or they can be tackled as separate sections in a pattern which may suit the reader.

Each study is divided up in the following way:

Reading

You need to begin by reading the chapter and verses mentioned at the start of each study. Sometimes it is helpful to read the verses in more than one version of the Bible to gain a better understanding of what the passage is saying. Before reading the Bible, it is good to develop the habit of spending a few minutes in prayer, asking God—by the Holy Spirit—to speak into your life.

Having read the passage, it would be helpful to you to spend time thinking over what you have just read—and perhaps writing down some of the thoughts that occur as you have gone over the verses.

Think through

This part is designed to get you thinking. I have tried to explain the basic meaning of the reading as well as applying some spiritual principles that can be drawn from it. Again, it is useful to write down the things that God says to you as you are reading. This section usually gives other Bible passages that you can look up and consider. This may well lead you to turn to other parts of the Bible as you think over the issues that are dealt with.

Workout

Christian truth is never meant to be left hanging in mid-air. This part is included to help you to apply the meaning of the Bible reading in your life today. If you are working through this book on your own you may wish to write down your responses to the questions that are asked. For those using the book as members of a Bible study group, we suggest that these questions could form the basis of your group sharing time. This means, of course, that each member will need to have thought about their personal response to the questions before sharing them with the others in the group.

From our own experience in group Bible studies, it is good not to become too tied down to the questions in a book. Learn to share together the ways in which God has been helping you to understand his word in relation to your everyday life.

Prayer

There is a brief prayer at the end of each study as you respond to what God has been saying to you. The prayers are short and relate directly to the issues raised in the study. You may wish to extend the prayers as, in your own words, you respond to God's truth.

PS

The studies conclude with a PS—sometimes a few verses from the Bible, a part of a song or hymn, or simply a quote to help fix the study in your mind. It is always good to come away from studying the Bible with one thing that sums up what God has been saying to you.

You may well have your own PS to add. Once again, it is helpful to write it down before it is forgotten.

To use this book on your own or as part of a group you need a Bible, something to write with and something to write on—plus time to be alone with God. Above all else, you need the help of the Holy Spirit. Jesus promised that the Holy Spirit will guide us into truth. Do not take that promise for granted—without his help we cannot begin to understand or apply the message of the Bible to our lives.

I

Teachability

Reading
2 Chronicles 10:1–19

Think through

Some months ago I had got angry with one of my children and, without a doubt, my reaction had been 'over the top'. Feeling bad about it all day, I knew I had to get things right with my five-year-old son. I apologized and asked for forgiveness. 'That's all right, Dad,' he replied in a matter-of-fact way. 'We all make mistakes!' With something approaching a lump in my throat and a suppressed giggle I realized that the two of us had learned something that day about the heart of God. Confession of failure makes you a candidate for help.

Rehoboam was a young king determined to make a good start. He had to fill his father's shoes and found them a few sizes too big.

The people sent a delegation to the King hoping that he would be more understanding than his father, Solomon. For years the wealth and splendid building projects that had made Solomon famous had been accomplished on the backs of the people. They wanted

17

some space and they asked the new King to give it to them.

Rehoboam asked for time to consider their request and then sought advice on the answer he should give. The people he turned to came up with totally different replies. The palace officials who had been with his father for years gave Rehoboam some sound advice: treat the people with kindness and relax the taxes and work-laws a little. Such a move would be good public relations, and the people would respond well.

Rehoboam's young friends who, like him, were enjoying their first taste of power advised the very opposite. They didn't possess the years of experience that Solomon's advisers had, but they were, without doubt, enthusiastic, creative and determined to make a success of their jobs. They told Rehoboam to reject the people's request and tell them that his intention was to be a firmer King than his father had been. If they thought they had had a hard time with Solomon, they would find Rehoboam even tougher!

The King considered the conflicting advice and chose the hard line—probably because friends' views always carry more weight. In taking the tough approach, Rehoboam made the worst decision of his life. The result was total disaster. Civil war broke out and the kingdom of Israel was divided into two rival states of second-rate importance. David and Solomon had built up a prosperous and influential nation, and with a stupid, reckless decision Rehoboam threw it all away.

Teachability is an important quality to develop. To be teachable means that you are willing to learn as well as to listen. Rehoboam would certainly have benefited from a crash course on the subject.

But being teachable is not fashionable in 1980s Britain, and within our churches we have our own brand of I'm-right-everybody-else-is-wrong. The gospel *is* about certainties but the problem is that we sometimes feel that gives us the right to pronounce on every subject under the sun and never be wrong. We sometimes confuse Peter's advice, 'Always be prepared to give an answer to everyone who asks you to give the reasons for the hope that you have' (1 Peter 3:15), with giving instant opinions on every issue on earth.

The word 'disciple' means someone who learns or is teachable. And learning means, from time to time, making mistakes and growing because of them. It means changing your mind, seeing something in a new light or taking advice that you would rather not listen to.

* Who does the teaching? God—it is part of his growing plan for our lives (John 15:1–2).

* How does he teach us? Through his word, other believers and the experience of the ups and downs of life (Hebrews 12:5ff).

* How can I learn to be teachable? Here are three positive responses:

Humility

As twentieth-century people we are a proud bunch. We can fly at two-and-a-half times the speed of sound, split the atom and walk in space. That is why God seems hard to find to people who want to confine him to an equation or examine him in a test-tube. The Bible warns: 'God opposes the proud but gives grace to the humble' (1 Peter 5:5). Sir Isaac Newton, the father of modern science and a God-fearing man, could teach us all something about humility through his words:

> I do not know what I may appear to the world, but to myself I seem to have been only a little boy playing on the seashore and diverting myself in now and then finding a smoother

pebble or a prettier shell than ordinary, whilst the great Ocean of Truth lay all undiscovered before me.

Willingness to learn

It is not failure to admit that you don't have all the answers. Trading in certainties can make us slick if we are not too careful. If we are truly disciples of Jesus then we are in the learning business—and his teaching comes through unlikely channels. The story of Rehoboam is *not* saying that old heads are always the wisest, but it warns us to be ready to hear God from surprising sources.

Admitting mistakes

One of the proofs that you are teachable is that you are willing to admit when you have got it wrong. None of us find it easy to own up to that!

Teachability may make me feel vulnerable, but in the long run it makes me strong.

Workout

1. As we've read, our teaching needs to come from God—through his word, other believers and everyday experiences in life. What have you learned from God during this last week? Are you beginning to apply those lessons in your life now?

2. No age group, race, sex or denomination has the monopoly on hearing from God. Would you be willing to 'hear God' through any channel—or do you set limits in your own mind on those he will use and those he won't?

3. Pride in our opinions, status, upbringing, education, church background, etc, can hinder our growth as Christians. Are there any areas in your life where you can't or won't be taught?

Two verses about learning and growing are:

1 Samuel 3:19: 'The Lord was with Samuel as he grew up, and he let none of his words fall to the ground.'

Luke 2:52: 'And Jesus grew in wisdom and stature, and in favour with God and men.'

We are God's children and, in one sense, our growing up is in our own hands because it involves listening, learning and living.

That growing process won't finish (or shouldn't anyway) this side of heaven. Our God always has something to teach us... if we're willing to learn.

Prayer

Dear Father, thank you that you have so much to teach us; so many wonderful lessons that you want to share with us. May we know the joy of hearing your voice, a willingness and eagerness to learn from you and the strength to really live for you by the power of your Holy Spirit. Amen.

PS

My son, if you accept my words
    and store up my commands within you,
turning your ear to wisdom
    and applying your heart to understanding,
and if you call out for insight
    and cry aloud for understanding,
and if you look for it as for silver
    and search for it as for hidden treasure,
then you will understand the fear of the Lord
    and find the knowledge of God.
For the Lord gives wisdom,
    and from his mouth come knowledge and
    understanding.

(Proverbs 2:1–6)

SECTION 1

David—
Running the Race

2

The Heart of the Matter

Reading

1 Samuel 16:1–23

Think through

The car looked fine from the outside—sun roof, alloy wheels, cloth trim, plus a fitted stereo. The advertisement had read: '*Immaculate, one (lady) owner, low mileage. Bargain price £350.*' The price should have given the game away. One look under the bonnet and it was a different story. The car was in need of the mechanic's equivalent of the last rites. The bodywork *was* immaculate—but from a distance. Close up it was all too obvious that the rot had set in.

In these next few chapters we are going to take a look at the life of David who is known in the Bible as 'the man after God's own heart'. His first appearance in Scripture tells us a great deal about the sort of person that God can use.

King Saul had blown it. Instead of obeying God he decided to do his own thing which, as always, ended in disaster. God rejected Saul as King and sent Samuel on a special mission to anoint his replacement. Samuel was God's spokesman to the nation of Israel and he had an impressive track record. But he still had lessons to learn. In God's school none of us takes the 'L' plates off this side of heaven.

Samuel was sent to the home of Jesse, a wealthy landowner who lived in Bethlehem with the message that one of his sons was to replace Saul as King. Samuel naturally thought that the eldest son—Eliab—was the man for the job. After all, culture dictated that the first-born was to be treated as the most important and, besides, he looked a 'Grade A' type! Enter Samuel's important lesson:

> But the Lord said to Samuel, 'Do not consider his appearance or his height, for I have rejected him. The Lord does not look at the things man looks at. Man looks at the outward appearance, but the Lord looks at the heart' (1 Samuel 16:7).

The prophet passed along the line of seven sons, only to discover to his horror that none of them was the man that God had chosen. Anxious to double-check his guidance he asked Jesse if he had any more sons. The youngest—David—had been left looking after the sheep, as he was considered the least important to meet the great man Samuel. When David was eventually ushered in, the old prophet immediately knew in his heart that this young lad was the man God had marked out to lead the nation of Israel.

From this passage of the Bible we discover a number of important principles that we would do well to get hold of:

THE HEART OF THE MATTER

1. God's choice is not always man's choice

In a society where how you look, what you wear and how much you own seem to count for everything, it is shattering to see that these things mean nothing in God's eyes. The oldest, strongest and seemingly most gifted in David's family was by-passed by God, who was far more concerned about the contents than the package.

We need to give up trying to impress people all of the time and concentrate our efforts on pleasing God. And if you feel useless or realize that you wouldn't even make the qualifying rounds of *Mastermind*—don't give up! God is not locked into the success syndrome that man has designed—it's what is on the inside that matters to him.

2. It's your heart that counts

What had God seen in David's life that pleased him?

* He had room for God: David had found that getting alone often with God gave him the sort of strength that really matters (Psalm 1:1–3).

* He had love for God: Take a look at the Psalms which David wrote that express a deep relationship with God. For example Psalm 63:1.

* He had faith in God: David had proved that he could be trusted to be trusted. God was about to let him loose on a nation not just a flock of sheep (Psalm 31:14–15).

How is your heart? No, I am not suggesting unhealthy introspection, but it is an important question. Have you got the sort of heart that David had? A heart that is after God will never go unsatisfied (see Matthew 5:8).

3. We need the anointing of the Holy Spirit

In the Old Testament, anointing with oil was reserved for three special groups of people: the king, the priest and the prophet. It marked them out as being reserved to serve God and was seen as a symbol of the power of God's Spirit resting on their lives (1 Samuel 16:13).

In the New Testament, receiving the Holy Spirit is seen as the indispensable mark of the Christian. We need him *within* us (John 3:5) and we need him *upon* us (Acts 1:8). Without his anointing on our lives anything that we try to accomplish in our own strength will be a waste of time.

God will give us the anointing that we need to serve him if we fulfil his twin conditions of obedience and faith.

Someone once commented that if the Holy Spirit was removed all over Britain next Sunday, 95% of Christians wouldn't notice the difference! Make certain that you serve God in his power and not your own.

4. If you are God's person—his fruit will be seen in your life

Verse 18 of 1 Samuel 16 gives what has to be one of the best character references in the Bible! The mark of a man or woman of God is a life that is like Jesus. Fruit takes time to grow and God sometimes allows hard knocks to come into our lives. This is his way of pruning us and making us more fruitful.

David was producing the fruit of a life given to God:

* Discipline: Homework, study assignments and getting to work on time may not seem to have anything to do with being a Christian, but they do matter. Discipline in the practical, everyday things is tremendous training for serving God.

* Character: David was recognized as a courageous, strong and wise person. Don't waste time worrying about your reputation; concentrate on building your character in a way that pleases God, and let him take care of your reputation.

* Faith: If you bump into someone carrying a bucket filled to the brim with water, the chances are that some of it will spill over. Whatever fills you 'spills over' when you meet people. If you are filled with faith and love for God it will show, and if you are full of yourself that will be obvious too.

God can use *anyone*. It is not your ability that counts, but your availability. It is your heart that matters, and if you make sure that is right—the possibilities are eternal.

Workout

1. We've read about the qualities God saw in David's life that pleased him. How do you match up with God's checklist?

2. God may not want you to be a king! David started with sheep and you may need to start with giving out hymnbooks before you can lead the worship in church. The point is, do you allow God to use you and do you believe he can use you in any job/task/area of ministry, however humble that may be?

3. How does the time you take preparing your outward appearance and building up your image or reputation compare with the time you spend with God? (It may help you to run through a typical day's timetable for the true answer!)

Take some time to consider this comment: 'Our disqualifications are often God's qualifications!' It's an exciting truth that God can use us in spite of ourselves. Just think of the possibilities!

Prayer

Thank you Father for making me as I am. Help me to be faithful in whatever you give me to do, so that you can trust me with more as time goes on. Help me to keep my priorities right—in spending time with you, getting to know you and love you more, and being completely available for you to use. Amen.

PS

God is more concerned with the contents than the package!

3

The Bigger They Are,
The Harder They Fall

Reading

1 Samuel 17:1–58

Think through

Question: What has the Bible story of David and Goliath
   to do with glue-sniffing, over-eating, or masturbation?
Answer: Everything! That is, if you are prepared to take
   the word of God seriously as God's guidebook for
   living.

Sadly, we have relegated the story of the boy versus
the giant to the memory banks. It takes us back to far off
days in dusty Sunday School classrooms, freezing to
death and watching the dark green paint peeling off the
walls. For some of us, David and Goliath have become
about as relevant as the story of Jack and the Beanstalk.
Riveting stuff when you're five years old, but when it
comes to the *real* world....

The story, however, is not a folk legend but a
remarkable, factual account of how God led Israel to
defeat the hostile Philistine nation through the spiritual

strength of one young man.

It is all too easy for us to live as defeated Christians. We all know what it is to be swamped by temptation and then be trapped in the living hell of knowing what is right and feeling powerless to do it. Blow the dust off the story of David and Goliath because there is much in it to help us.

David didn't beat Goliath with proof-texts but by trusting in God's power to help when he was at his weakest. We all face 'giants' every day of our lives. Often we turn tail and run or—worse still—lie down and play dead. But that is not God's intention for our lives. He is 'able to keep you from falling' (Jude 24) and that is exactly what he wants to do. Take a look at the way David faced Goliath and relate it to the 'giants' you are facing.

1. He was willing to fight (1 Samuel 17:26, 32)

David recognized that Goliath was doing more than challenging Israel—he was defying God. Evil (or sin) is anything or anyone who challenges God's right to rule. That is exactly what Goliath was doing and David was willing to fight that challenge.

We live in a hostile world where spiritual forces which are opposed to the living God are at work. Those forces challenge his right to rule. If you are following King Jesus, that makes your life part of the battleground!

The question is, do you want to be a soldier who wins or a coward who runs? Graham Kendrick has a powerful song which has the recurring line 'God put a fighter in me'. That is the sort of determination that we need and it is a desire that must be expressed in our prayers. Refuse to run away any longer. Ask God to make you a fighter, and a fighter who wins.

2. He faced today's problems on the basis of yesterday's experience (1 Samuel 17:34–35)

David was not totally wet behind the ears! His experience in looking after sheep had allowed God to teach him valuable lessons. He had courage, moral strength, and he can't have been any seven-stone weakling either as his previous match record with a lion and a bear prove! His experience of God's help in the past gave him faith for God's power for the present.

Whenever Satan attacks a Christian one of his first targets is the memory. He is an expert in trying to blank out our recollections of God's help in the past. That is why we often end up looking at a problem and convincing ourselves that it is the biggest 'giant' we have ever come across. We forget that God has stepped in many times in the past and dealt with bigger problems than the ones we face today.

Thanksgiving is a great antidote to satanic attacks on the memory. Today's lessons are tomorrow's memories —don't forget them.

3. He refused to rely on the best human weapons (1 Samuel 17:38–40)

There is something almost comical about the picture of David trying on Saul's armour. There was quite a difference in their ages and, without a doubt, in their sizes too! David flatly refused to face Goliath weighed down with the King's armour.

Human logic suggested that it was ridiculous for David to go out to fight without wearing armour. But his victory over Goliath did not depend on him using the latest weapons. Goliath was a dead man before David left the tent. What killed Goliath ultimately was not a sword or a stone—but spiritual authority.

Paul reminded the Corinthian church that 'the

weapons we fight with are not the weapons of the world'
(2 Corinthians 10:4). Prayer/Bible study/being committed to a local body of believers/honest, open
fellowship—these are not optional extras for the extra-
keen. They are part of the armoury that God has given
us. We must *use* the weapons he has given us.

4. *He faced Goliath with absolute faith in God (1 Samuel 17:45–47)*

Goliath was mad when he saw that the Israelites had sent
a boy to do a man's job. He hurled curses and insults.
David's response was to stand against him with calm
spiritual authority and say: 'I come against you in the
name of the Lord Almighty, the God of the armies of
Israel, whom you have defied' (verse 45). David was not
relying on his own strength but on God's. We dare not
do any less in the battles that we face.

In his preface to *The Screwtape Letters* C. S. Lewis
warned of two opposite errors that people fall into
concerning satanic powers: 'One is to disbelieve their
existence. The other is to believe and to feel an excessive
and unhealthy interest in them.'

A third danger is to become so over-familiar with
satanic forces that we underestimate their subtlety. Satan
is for real. His power (although limited) is real. Beware
of treating him as a joke.

During World War Two, Field Marshall Montgomery
led his troops to victory in the African desert. During the
campaign he kept on display in his room a photograph of
the German Commander, Rommel. The reason? He
never wanted to forget what his enemy looked like.

God will lead you to victory if you trust him. *His*
power is the greatest. 'The one who is in you is greater
than the one who is in the world' (1 John 4:4).

5. *He gave God the glory (1 Samuel 17:47)*

David remembered that the battle and the victory belonged to God, and that left no room for personal bragging. Pride is a nasty sin. It creeps up on you unawares and grabs you by the throat before you realize its presence. One minute you can be crying out to God for help and the next feeling pleased with *yourself* at how *you* handled the problem.

But however far we may have travelled in the Christian life, it's because of God's grace. Whatever we have received of any lasting worth is through his love. 'For who makes you different from anyone else? What do you have that you did not receive? And if you did receive it, why do you boast as though you did not?' (1 Corinthians 4:7).

The book of Psalms is full of David's songs. Worship songs that he wrote in every mood of life. Through all of them comes a sense of his deep gratitude to God, because David never forgot to give the glory to the One to whom it truly belongs.

Crash!! The door flew open and in rushed a hurricane on legs. The ten-year-old terror of the Sunday School was home and hungry. 'What did you learn today, son?' his father asked. 'It was great, Dad!' he gasped, as he mounted his assault on the tea table. 'We learned all about David and this big guy called Goliath. He was puttin' it about a bit, so David sorted 'im out. He softened the other army up with a few B52s dropping several hundred tons, then they brought in the anti-personnel rockets and wiped out the whole of the Philistine forces with a frontal assault by a commando regiment, backed up with a couple of tank support columns!'

'Er...are you *sure* that's what your teacher told

you?' enquired his incredulous father. 'Well, not exactly, Dad...but if I told it the way she did, you'd *never* believe it!'

Truth is often stranger than fiction. And God's truth, when taken in and applied to your life, can teach you how to handle 'giants'—and survive to see them fall flat on their faces.

Workout

1. What are the 'giants' in your life? Have you tried to face them or have you just conceded defeat? Name them before God (it would probably help to write them down) and start to rely on *his* strength to overcome them.

2. It's easy to see that Goliath was defying God, but is it as obvious to realize that your 'giants' defy God too?

3. How does God want you to fight these 'giants' and what weapons has he given you? There are a few helpful 'stones' of truth listed below to help you in the battle.

* *Temptation:* 1 Corinthians 10:13; Ephesians 6:10–18; 1 John 1:9.

* *Fear:* Psalm 91:1; Proverbs 3:5–6; 1 John 4:18.

* *Doubt:* Matthew 11:1–6; Hebrews 11:1–40; Psalm 139:1–24.

* *Opposition:* Matthew 5:11–12; Psalm 27:1–14; 1 Corinthians 1:27; Romans 8:31–39.

God *is* concerned with the 'giants' in your life (even if you think that everyone else would see them as 'midgets'), but it's no use just standing back and waiting for him to do everything, because he waits for our willingness to fight before he arms us! As we take our stand and fight so God will equip us.

Prayer

Dear Father, help me to recognize those areas in my life that defy your lordship. Thank you that you didn't wait until I was perfect to show me you loved me. I *am* your child and I know I can trust you as I fight these 'giants' that are taking my attention from you. Thank you that you don't send me out to battle on my own— you are with me and you give me your Spirit with all the power I will ever need. Hallelujah! Amen.

PS

When your enemy presses in hard, do not fear,
The battle belongs to the Lord.
Take courage, my friend, your redemption is near,
The battle belongs to the Lord.
  We sing glory, honour, power and strength to the Lord
  Power and strength to the Lord.

From Jamie Owens-Collins, *The Battle Belongs to the Lord*, copyright © Fairhill Music/Word Music (UK) 1985. Used by permission.

4

With a Little Help from My Friends

Reading

1 Samuel 18:1–16

Think through

As the Beatles sang about 'getting by with a little help from my friends' the world went crazy. Half were Beatle-maniacs celebrating the release of another smash hit and the other half were those who claimed the lyrics were extolling drug-taking and encouraging people to pop pills.

Drugs may seem like 'friends' to help you get by but they have no answers for man's deepest needs, as many have tragically discovered to their cost.

People need people, not pills. And if you are going to survive and grow strong as a Christian you will soon discover how much you need *real* fellowship. It is one of God's greatest gifts to his church. I'm not talking about the limp-handshake-do-stay-after-the-service-for-a-cup -of-tea-and-a-biscuit idea of fellowship, but the real thing. *Koinonia* is a great New Testament word for

WITH A LITTLE HELP FROM MY FRIENDS

fellowship, which carries the meaning of 'sharingship'—
and we could all do with a richer experience of that.

One of the strengths in David's life was a deep
friendship that developed between him and King Saul's
son, Jonathan. Strangely enough the friendship grew
despite the fact that the two men had every reason to be
sworn enemies. After all, Jonathan was next in line to
the throne and in God's plan David was about to push
him out of the picture. In 1 Samuel 18 we begin to get an
understanding of how the relationship grew.

1. It was deep

'Jonathan became one in spirit with David, and he loved
him as himself' (1 Samuel 18:1).

Sadly, in today's society, a deep relationship between
two people of the same sex leads some people to the
assumption that 'they must be queers'.

The Bible makes no such suggestion. It is obvious that
God allowed the bond to grow between them and their
friendship helped them both to discover more about him
and his purpose for their lives.

We need to take time to develop the sort of friendships
that will help us to grow in our Christian lives. Not
unhealthy exclusive relationships, but deep friendships
that count for God.

2. It was costly

King Saul was an insanely jealous man. The friendship
between his son and the rival to the throne incensed him.
In 1 Samuel 20:30 we read:

> Saul's anger flared up at Jonathan and he said to him, 'You
> son of a perverse and rebellious woman! Don't I know that
> you have sided with the son of Jesse to your own shame and
> to the shame of the mother who bore you?'

The relationship between David and Jonathan was not superficial, it was costly. It cost Jonathan a great deal to maintain the friendship, but it was a price he was willing to pay.

Real fellowship is always costly. It takes *time* to develop a relationship of value. It takes *honesty*—which can sometimes be very painful. It takes *love*, and if it is the genuine article, it makes you vulnerable.

3. *It was built on loyalty*

'Jonathan made a covenant with David because he loved him as himself' (1 Samuel 18:3). This covenant was a solemn agreement, made in God's presence, that their friendship would be one of loyalty and trust. Jonathan gave David his royal robes, along with his sword, bow and belt (1 Samuel 18:4), as tokens of his willingness to give himself in loyal friendship. Such a gesture to modern, western minds seems odd, but in the culture in which they were living, personal belongings were held to possess and express something of a person's whole being. The gesture was a rich, expressive symbol of the giving of one person in total commitment to another.

How much do we give of ourselves in friendship? What about loyalty? If someone opens up to us about their innermost thoughts can they feel safe that we will not tell anyone else? How trustworthy are we?

4. *It was God-centred*

The most telling verse about the value of the friendship comes in 1 Samuel 23:16: 'Jonathan went to David at Horesh and helped him to find strength in God.' David had reached one of the lowest points in his life. Everything was crumbling around his ears: Saul was out to kill him and he was running scared. Jonathan turned up just in time, and because their friendship had developed on a spiritual level he was able to help David find strength in God when he needed it most.

We all face times when we feel cut off and God seems to be a million miles away. And it is at times like these when the value of our friendships are proved. Most of us have a circle of Christians that we can call friends, but we need to learn how to take those friendships beyond a superficial level to form relationships that are God-centred.

On a building site it's the easiest thing in the world to pinch a couple of bricks that are lying around on their own. But you try stealing a wall! Because the bricks are bonded together they find mutual support and strength. On our own we are vulnerable, but bonded to others we are protected.

The relationship between David and Jonathan has often been taken up and spiritualized as a picture (or type) of the Lord Jesus Christ and an individual believer. Many Christians have seen in these chapters helpful illustrations of the way in which we need to be committed to the Lord in loyalty and faithfulness. As good as this may be, it does take us away from the important lesson to be learned about human friendship: *if you are going to survive in the battle you need to build relationships that count*.

Deep Christian friendships don't just happen—they need to be worked at. Here are some ways to help you start laying some foundations:

* *Time:* It is amazingly easy to waste time drinking coffee, sitting around listening to music and chatting about nothing in particular. There's nothing wrong with relaxing, but learn to make time to create friendships that God can use. Be willing to sit and listen and give people time to open up about their joys and hurts.

* *Prayer:* Learn to pray with your friends. There's no need to feel embarrassed or to create a false atmosphere.

Pray naturally about the things you have been talking through. Pray for the people you know. Pray for your church. Often Christians who are scared of a large prayer meeting have found it easier to 'break the sound barrier' in a one-to-one prayer time.

* *Sharing:* This is probably one of the most overworked and misused words in the Christian vocabulary! Real sharing can often hurt because it means opening ourselves up to others. You can only do that in an atmosphere of love and security, when you know that what you share will be held in guarded confidence. Learn to share, but beware of the dangers of talking too much. Some of us would grow a lot quicker if we spent more time listening to other people's needs instead of giving our own pet problems yet another airing.

* *Honesty:* This is always the best policy in a valuable friendship which God can bless. Be prepared to take your mask off and be yourself. No one can open themselves up fully to a large group of people (nor would it be wise to do so), but a friendship with God at the centre is one where you can learn the value of openness. This in turn opens the way for friends to be honest with you, and we all need putting right from time to time. It is easy to have 'blind spots' of which we are unaware. Have you got someone that you love and trust enough for them to be that honest with you?

* *Faithfulness:* Putting people right when they are wrong is one thing, but the other side of the coin is to go on loving them and remaining a committed friend in spite of their faults. A true Christian friend won't blow hot and cold, but should be willing to stay with you when the going gets tough.

* *Sacrifice:* We all know John 3:16 by heart (don't we?), but how many of us are familiar with *1* John 3:16? 'This is

how we know what love is: Jesus Christ laid down his life for us. And we ought to lay down our lives for our brothers.'

It's easy to read, but difficult to practise. Be willing to *give* instead of just *take*. Even as you read these words you may have been saying to yourself: 'If only I had friends like that.' Instead, try saying: 'Lord make me a friend like that.'

The best way to deal with the problem of selfish living is to get on with a bit of sacrificial giving.

* *Freedom:* We have probably all seen 'exclusive' friendships and the sort of damage they can cause. A truly God-centred relationship is open at both ends and in it we are willing to receive from others and to give to others too. If God has built a relationship then other people won't threaten it. We don't need the sort of mind-control relationships that are practised by some of the cults, but we do need friendships that have purpose and that help us to reach out to minister to the needs of others.

I will always be grateful for two young men who came to me when I was just starting out in Christian ministry. I didn't know either of them very well, but they expressed a desire to meet with me on a regular basis for prayer and encouragement. They could see I was going to need it! Both had young families and demanding jobs, which meant that the only time we could meet was 6 o'clock in the morning! Slowly, God began to build a relationship between us which to me, at times, was like a liferaft in the middle of a storm. The relationship has grown, and so have we.

Alan Redpath has written of the friendship of David and Jonathan in these words:

When I think of that story my heart is stirred by a desire not

43

only that I might have a Jonathan in my life—that is surely very wonderful, but very selfish—but also that I might find a David somewhere to whom I could be a Jonathan.

We all need friendships—especially ones that can help us grow in God. Ask him to create relationships that count, but don't simply pray: 'Lord, give me a Jonathan.' Start out by praying: 'Lord, *make* me a Jonathan.'

Workout

1. The name 'Jonathan' means 'The Lord has given'. What a fabulous honour and privilege to be a Jonathan— someone that God has given to somebody else. What qualities has God given you to share with other people? Are you willing to share yourself in that way?

2. Read through the hallmarks of deep Christian friendships again: time, prayer, sharing, honesty, faithfulness, sacrifice and freedom. As you read through those qualities is there someone you can think of that you would be able to be a Jonathan to? (Don't forget...you're not looking at this for what you'll get out of it!)

Prayer

Dear Father, thank you for my Christian friends. Please forgive me for so often concentrating on negative things, like how others annoy me, how they take me for granted. (I wonder how they see me?) To follow your example I need to learn to give and give again. Please help me to do that. Help me to be a 'Jonathan'. Amen.

PS

Here are some lines from a song by Phil Potter:

Some people say, 'I'm better off on my own,'
But God said, 'It's not good for man to be alone.'
So why are we so independent
And sometimes so cold?

Some people never would agree
That they really need your company.
But you get nowhere until you learn to share
Got to learn to laugh and cry with me.

Some people live in their own dreams,
'God helps those who help themselves', or so it seems.
But you get nowhere until you learn to share
Got to learn to laugh and cry with me.

Now when I'm feeling that I could run a mile,
There's so much meaning in your peaceful smile.
And you lift that shield of faith up for me
When you help me rest awhile.

Phil Potter, *Laugh and Cry with Me* copyright © Thankyou Music 1980. Used by permission.

5

Breaking It and Making It

Reading

2 Samuel 11:1–27; 12:1–25

Think through

The headlines screamed: 'Vicar runs off with choirmistress—sex scandal shocks village.'

We've all read such headlines at one time or another. And while the world gloats over the gory details, maybe you've felt a stab of sadness that another Christian has made a mess of his life and the name of Jesus gets dragged in the mud.

Perhaps it has happened in your own church. Like a young friend of mine who wrote recently explaining that the pastor had resigned due to 'marital problems which involved another family in the church'. Behind the euphemisms lies tragedy: broken promises, broken homes, broken testimonies, broken lives. When Christian leaders fall they make a lot of noise.

When people we trust and respect fall into sin the big temptation is to write Christianity off as a sham. And that is exactly what Satan wants us to do. If our Christian lives are based on just an experience, or if we have an unhealthy 'cult hero' attitude towards our leaders, then we could easily find our faith severely shaken. That is why it is so important to make certain we are building on the solid foundation of God's truth and not on other people.

Our last look at David's life is frank. The Bible paints no 'hearts and flowers' pictures of its great men and women. David—'a man after God's heart'—blew it, and the word of God makes no attempt to hide that.

1. David's sin (2 Samuel 11:1–27)

How on earth did David get tangled up in this messy spider's web of sin? How could a man of God commit adultery and then engineer a murder to cover his tracks?

* *He took his eyes off God.* The rot had set in long before his roof-top walk (verse 2). David had grown flabby in his spiritual life. He had drunk in too much of the world's thinking. Immorality in the world of his day was rife. Kings were all-powerful and could have what or *whom* they wanted. David had forgotten he was not just any king; that he was God's king ruling God's people.

'Do not conform any longer to the pattern of this world, but be transformed by the renewing of your mind' (Romans 12:2). It is vitally important for us to allow God to shape our thoughts. If we are just a church-on-Sunday person then how much input does God have in our lives? Maybe one thirty-minute sermon is the total amount of God's truth we take in for a whole week. The other 167½ hours are crammed full of influences that are all to do with 'the pattern of the world'.

* *No one is immune from temptation.* David had let his guard drop. He was lulled into thinking he was safe from attack. If he could have been shown all that was to

follow, I have no doubt he would not have looked twice at Bathsheba.

* *Laziness breeds sin.* David had stayed behind while his army went off to fight (verse 1). He had time on his hands, and that is when we can be most vulnerable. David's place was at the head of his army, but instead he decided to take things easy and stay at home.

Learn to use your time well. And when you do have time to spare, don't waste it, spend it! One of the best defences against temptation is a disciplined life with God at the centre.

* *It starts in your mind.* Josh McDowell describes the mind as 'your most important sex organ'—and he's right! If the deed really is the child of the thought, then David should have strangled this particular daydream at birth.

The best place to deal with temptation is in the mind. David, instead of turning his heart to God in that moment of weakness, let his own appetites rule him.

'Go on, enjoy yourself'...'It won't hurt anyone'... 'What's wrong with a bit of fun?' We've all heard those voices at times, but what hollow lies they are—as David discovered to his cost.

* *Sin goes from bad to worse.* Read from verse 4 to the end of the chapter. What began as an idle fantasy ended up in disaster. David sinned against God, the nation, Bathsheba, Uriah (her husband), Joab (whom he dragged into the sordid affair) and himself. Sin is a wild horse that is hard to handle once it is let loose.

I sat in a prison a few years ago, talking to a guy who was a professing Christian whose whole life had been shattered. How did it all go wrong? 'One thing just led to another,' he told me.

As we traced back his painful story together he could see clearly where the problem had started—in refusing to be honest with himself, with others and, most of all, with God.

2. David's discovery (2 Samuel 12:1–12)

You can never do a cover-up job on God. 'You may be sure that your sin will find you out' (Numbers 32:23).

Nathan, God's spokesman, came to David with what seemed like a story of injustice. David reacted with understandable anger, until Nathan delivered the killer punch: '*You* are the man' (verse 7).

David could have tried to make excuses. He could have had Nathan killed for daring to confront him. Instead, he became a broken man as he humbled himself before God. If you want a real insight into what was going on inside him, read Psalm 51 where David pours out his heart in repentance to God. Brokenness always leads to healing and forgiveness. How do *you* react to discipline? What do you do if someone points out an area of need in your life? We all need Nathans who are honest and faithful enough to bring God's word to our lives when we need it most.

3. David's recovery (2 Samuel 12:13–25)

God's grace is incredible! When we confess and repent, he promises to forgive and forget. But we often have to live with the consequences of rebellion against God. The child conceived by Bathsheba died. David's son, Absalom, ultimately turned against his father and led a rebel army. Many of the seeds of that division were sown through David's adultery and murder.

God's mercy is real, and so is his justice. If you stress one at the expense of the other, you don't get a true picture of God—you end up with a caricature.

My children love to show me their pictures, but it is embarrassing when I can't 'guess who this is, Daddy'! Children have a tendency to draw people either with huge heads and tiny bodies or huge bodies and tiny heads—they have no sense of proportion.

It is the same with some Christians who stress God's love and forgiveness, but never mention his holiness, righteousness or justice. Check *your* vision of God with the biblical version.

The lesson from David's life is clear. God showed his grace and forgiveness to David and Bathsheba. The Bible, in a lovely phrase, tells us that God gave them another son, Solomon, and 'the Lord loved him' (verse 24). But at the same time, the glory of David's kingdom and the stability and peace of his rule were never the same again. His family was soon divided and David had to run for his life from Absalom, his own son. You can't play fast and loose with God—it doesn't work.

Cabinet ministers, pastors, elders, youth leaders—no one is immune from temptation. That should not cause us to be cynical or scared. It simply reminds us of two important things:

* *Pray for your leaders*. Don't be fooled into thinking that they never have problems—they do. In fact, the pressures and temptations are even greater when you are in leadership. Cover them with prayer.

* *Keep your eyes on Jesus*. It is easy to fall into the trap of thinking, 'If they're not safe, neither am I!' The Bible gives us many reassuring promises: 'To him who is able to keep you from falling and to present you before his glorious presence without fault and with great joy...'(Jude 24).

As you run the race, keep your eyes on Jesus (Hebrews 12:1–3). If you do that then no matter what is happening all around you, you will be able to keep going.

Someone once wrote, 'Even the best of men are only, at best, men.' All of us have got feet of clay—and that includes Christian leaders. What makes the difference is keeping them firmly planted on the Rock (the one that doesn't roll!).

Workout

1. We've seen how David was a man after God's own heart; how he was a man of faith ready to face Goliath; how that deep relationship was built with Jonathan... and now, that David wasn't perfect. It's an important reminder for all of us. Take a look again at the section headed 'David's sin' and notice the downward spiral of sin. You can probably pinpoint a few examples in your own life that prove those points. Look prayerfully at each characteristic listed. Ask God to help you learn from the mistakes you've made in the past and give you strength and ability to resist the temptation to sin.

2. It's so easy to get caught up in gossiping—talking about others behind their backs and literally rejoicing when a fellow Christian gets involved in some scandal. Just think what that does to God's heart—you're talking about his child... and your brother or sister. Christians are human and within the Christian family we should be ready to defend not destroy. Pray for Christian leaders.

Prayer

Dear Father, there are so many lessons to be learned from David's life. Please help me to learn and to put those lessons into practice in my life. Help me to know the reality and strength of 'keeping my eyes on Jesus'. Amen.

PS

Create in me a pure heart, O God,
  and renew a steadfast spirit within me.

Do not cast me from your presence
    or take your Holy Spirit from me.
Restore to me the joy of your salvation
    and grant me a willing spirit, to sustain me.

                     (Psalm 51:10–12)

These things happened to them as examples and were written down as warnings for us, on whom the fulfilment of the ages has come. So, if you think you are standing firm, be careful that you don't fall! No temptation has seized you except what is common to man. And God is faithful; he will not let you be tempted beyond what you can bear. But when you are tempted, he will also provide a way out so that you can stand up under it (1 Corinthians 10:11–13).

SECTION 2

The Beatitudes— Christ-likeness

6

Beautiful Attitudes

Reading

Matthew 5:1–12

Think through

The camera zooms in over the palm trees swaying in the gentle breeze and across the sun-kissed beach. The hazy, soft-focus lens picks the couple out as they run, hand in hand, splashing through the glistening shallows. She— blonde, willowy, wistful and full of teeth. He—sharp, dark, rugged, with the statutory gold medallion adorning a chest that looks like a burst mattress. And all that to sell a box of chocolates!

The glossy magazines and the TV ads seem to pulverize us with their message. They feed us with their stereotype images of the 'beautiful woman' or the 'successful man', and suddenly we find ourselves caught in the Venus fly-trap of buying in the hope that by owning or using 'things' we will magically become the people they tell us we really want to be.

But who does God want us to be? As a Christian, who should we be imitating? Come to that, who do we most want to impress by our lives?

This, and the following four chapters, takes a look at the Beatitudes (or the beautiful attitudes, as someone once described them). We find them at the beginning of the Sermon on the Mount, and the word means 'to be blessed'. They tell us the sort of people God wants us to be and point to the liberating truth that he can actually make us those people.

The Sermon on the Mount forms a central part of the teaching ministry of the Lord Jesus Christ. Let's take a look at the background to the greatest sermon ever preached.

1. The preacher

Jesus Christ, the Son of God (verse 1).

2. The congregation

His disciples (verse 1). Jesus was not preaching to the world at large, but to his committed followers. You will never discover the power to live the life of a disciple unless you are one.

3. The place

On a mountainside (verse 1). Jesus sat down to teach— indicating that what he had to say had special weight and authority.

4. The time

Jesus had begun to preach that 'the kingdom of heaven is near' (Matthew 4:17). Whether the Sermon was given as one message, or a collection of the important truths Jesus taught over a period of time, Jesus is preaching about the kingdom which has arrived and of which he is King.

5. *The message*

In his Magna Carta of the kingdom, Jesus is declaring
how saved men and women can live—by the power of
God the Holy Spirit.

The Sermon comes in two parts:
   Christian character   Matthew 5:1–17
   Christian conduct   Matthew 5:17—7:29

The Beatitudes come in the first section where Jesus is
teaching about Christian character. From verses 3–11
each verse begins with the same word—'blessed'—but
what does it mean?

The Greek word used is *makarios* which means
'happy'. That is why some translations read, 'Happy
are ....' But that doesn't tell the whole story. The
English word 'happy' contains the root 'hap', which
simply means 'luck' or 'chance'. For many people, their
happiness depends on just that. If you pass an exam, get
a pay rise or a seat on the bus home, you are happy. But
Jesus brings us his joy and that joy is very special because
it does not come and go as outward circumstances change.

Jesus is teaching that his disciples are to be joyful
people. That joy comes when God's government comes
into a person's life. We discover God's joy when we
begin to see ourselves as we really are—poor in spirit—
because the kingdom of heaven is for those who discover
that the way down is the way up; to make ourselves low is
to be brought high.

God's kingdom does not consist of dark suits, dark
buildings and dark people, but 'righteousness, peace
and joy in the Holy Spirit' (Romans 14:17).

His joy is for those who discover:

* who they are   *the poor in spirit* (verse 3)
* that they've failed   *those who mourn* (verse 4)

* who's in charge	*the meek* (verse 5)
* where they're headed	*those who hunger and thirst for righteousness* (verse 6)
* how to forgive	*the merciful* (verse 7)
* how to keep clean	*the pure in heart* (verse 8)
* how to build bridges	*the peacemakers* (verse 9)
* how to keep going	*those who are persecuted* (verse 10)

In a world like ours that sort of talk doesn't make much sense. No wonder G. K. Chesterton wrote, 'On the first reading of the Sermon on the Mount you feel that it turns everything upside down.' Then he added, 'But the second time you read it you discover that it turns everything right side up.'

Take a few minutes to read through the list of qualities (verses 3–11) and allow God to speak to you about the areas in your life where you need the upside down (or right side up) principles of his rule to have a greater effect. Here are some important points to bear in mind:

1. They are about what we can be, not what we might be

Some (very sincere) Christians have said that the Beatitudes belong to the 'Kingdom Age' in the distant future. But each verse carries a promise that is for now, for example, 'Blessed are those who mourn for they shall be comforted.' God wants us to know the reality of that here and now.

2. They point us to the Holy Spirit's power

Strive all you can and you will never live up to those standards. We enter God's kingdom supernaturally and we live within it by the same resources. The Beatitudes are the fruit of the Holy Spirit (see Galatians 5:22–23).

3. They are for all disciples, not just some

We may be tempted to duck behind the excuse that this is a standard for the superstars of the faith; the rest of us must just do the best we can. Jesus makes no such distinctions. Anyway, none of these qualities depend on how well you can do, but how far you are prepared to let God go in your life.

4. Like pieces of a jigsaw they make a complete picture

In the same way that it is wrong to segregate the fruit of the Spirit, we can't break down the Beatitudes into bits. We need to study them as individual pieces of the jigsaw that fit together to make a picture of Jesus in our lives.

God has his stereotype that he wants you to fit, and that brings us back to where we started. But it's not a picture of a beach through a soft-focus lens, it's a picture of a towel and a bowl, in the shadow of a cross. It's called servanthood. And that means being like Jesus.

Workout

1. What's at the root of your happiness? Are those things passing, outward circumstances, or are they as a result of your relationship with God?

2. It's common to hear people praying to be more like Jesus—but rare to see it happen! Think through some of your attitudes, some of those hardened opinions that you hold. How do they compare with the 'beautiful attitudes' listed in Matthew 5? Do they reflect Jesus in your life?

3. 'But the fruit of the Spirit is love, joy, peace, patience, kindness, goodness, faithfulness, gentleness and self-control. Against such things there is no law' (Galatians 5:22–23). How much of the fruit of the Spirit are you showing in your life? Like the Beatitudes, this is

not a case of having 'the fruit of love' or 'the fruit of kindness' as one-offs. By the power of the Holy Spirit we should be exhibiting *all* the fruit in our lives.

Prayer

Dear Father, reading through the Beatitudes and the fruit of the Spirit I can see why I'm not as blessed as I could be! Please continue to work in my life and make me more like Jesus. Help me to learn to be a servant, and help me to realize, in seeing how far I have to go, that you *will* complete the work you have started in my life. Amen.

PS

> Jesus, you are changing me
>   by your Spirit you're making me like you.
> Jesus, you're transforming me
>   that your loveliness may be seen in all I do.
> You are the potter and I am the clay.
>   Help me to be willing to let you have your way.
> Jesus, you are changing me
>   as I let you reign supreme within my heart.

Marilyn Baker, *Jesus, you are changing me*, copyright © Word Music (UK) 1980. Used by permission.

> ... being confident of this, that he who began a good work in you will carry it on to completion until the day of Christ Jesus (Philippians 1:6).

7

Who Am I?

Readings

Matthew 5:3–4; Luke 18:9–14

Think through

'There were these two men.' As he began, the crowd went quiet. They liked his strange stories—always easy to follow, sometimes very funny, but always carrying a sting in the tail.

He continued, 'The two men were praying; one was a Pharisee and the other a tax collector.' Some of the crowd began to laugh because these were two groups of people who it was good to poke fun at. But the story was strangely serious. You remember how it ends. The Pharisee just prayed about himself, with a lot of spiritual pride, but the tax collector could not even look up and just murmured, 'God have mercy on me a sinner.'

What made the story really strange was Jesus saying that it was the tax collector who found peace with God and not the proud religious Pharisee, because 'everyone who exalts himself will be humbled, and he who humbles himself will be exalted' (Luke 18:14). You see, they both told God things he already knew—but only one told God what he really wanted to hear.

The parable about the two men praying is a picture of the first two Beatitudes. As we have already seen, the Beatitudes fit together like jigsaw pieces to make a picture of Jesus in our lives. Like building blocks, they go to make up a character that pleases God.

Learning who you are

'Blessed are the poor in spirit, for theirs is the kingdom of heaven' (Matthew 5:3).

What does it mean to be poor in spirit? Colourless, dull, unattractive? No! It means recognizing how spiritually bankrupt we are in ourselves—that we can only come to God as beggars, with empty hands.

The doorway into God's kingdom is narrow and also very low. You must stoop to get through it. Charles Spurgeon once said, 'The way to rise in the kingdom is to sink in ourselves.' That does not mean sinking into yourself so that you end up an introverted Christian whose motto for life begins 'poor me'. To be truly poor in spirit means seeing yourself as God sees you.

This little verse has sometimes been misused and abused—sometimes by people who have wanted to maintain the status quo by keeping the poor down. But Jesus is not saying that material poverty is a good thing. It is not a blessing to live in a slum or to see your children dying from malnutrition. The gospel commands us to wage war on such things.

Jesus is teaching that the first ingredient of a Christlike character is the ability to see how spiritually poor we really are. The Ancient Greeks used to say that the first step to real knowledge was to 'know thyself'. Do you see yourself as God sees you? Do you realize how spiritually poor you are? Have you discovered how rich Jesus is? For the poor in spirit the promise is, 'Theirs is the kingdom of heaven.'

Learning that you've failed

'Blessed are those who mourn, for they will be comforted' (Matthew 5:4).

The word 'mourn' is a strong one. It is used for the deep sorrow we feel when someone close to us dies. It means brokenness. But what did Jesus mean when he said, in effect, 'Happy are the unhappy'?

Mourning is the reaction we experience when we realize that we are poor in spirit. Jesus is speaking about the sorrow of repentance—brokenness before God at the sin in our lives and the sin that destroys and warps God's world. We need to learn more about brokenness. In order to receive the full blessing of forgiveness (and the joy that comes with it) we need to do more than say we are sorry. We need to feel sorry and we need to act sorry. That is what is meant in Matthew 3:8 where it says, 'Produce fruit in keeping with repentance.'

I was a witness in court some time ago. The detective in charge of the case was talking with me and I explained that I had spent time with the accused person and I felt that he was genuinely sorry for the crime he had committed.

The detective was hard but honest. 'Listen,' he said, 'I've been in this job a long time. There are two types of "sorry". Most people are saying, "I'm sorry I was caught," only a few mean, "I'm sorry I ever did it."'

That was the best exposition I have ever heard of 2 Corinthians 7:10: 'Godly sorrow brings repentance that leads to salvation and leaves no regret, but worldly sorrow brings death.'

Learning to share God's heart

Mourning means more than sorrow over sin in our own lives. It means entering into God's heart about sin in his world. Have you ever asked God what makes him angry

63

about our world, or what makes him sad? Prophets like
Amos, Ezekiel and Jeremiah knew the answers to those
questions. Take a look at what they discovered. If you
want to be God's person then you need to learn to share
his heart.

Some of us may feel confused. Surely Jesus brings joy,
happiness and laughter—not misery? But look at the
whole verse. The blessing of this Beatitude is that those
who mourn shall be comforted. Like the Prodigal Son
who came home admitting failure and received the kiss
of forgiveness. Like Jesus who wept over a lost city full
of lost people, and as Isaiah prophesied, 'After the
suffering of his soul, he will see the light of life and be
satisfied' (Isaiah 53:11).

People who are broken by God and put back together
by him *are* happy. The kingdom of God is a glorious,
mysterious mixture of tears and smiles, laughter and
weeping.

The consequence of not learning

I can think of a church where the people know very little
about being poor in spirit or mourning deeply over sin,
and as a result they have not entered into all the good
things that God has for them. They are an active bunch.
To the average visitor they have got a lot going for them,
but, tragically, they do not see themselves as God sees
them. Their attitude is, 'I am rich, I have acquired
wealth and do not need a thing.' The sad truth is that
they don't realize they are 'poor, blind and naked' and as
for being 'wretched and pitiful'...the thought had never
entered their heads!

God is about to spit them out of his mouth because
lukewarmness is such a sickening thing. You can read
God's assessment of the church at Laodicea in
Revelation 3:14–22. The sad thing is that if they had
been prepared to admit how poor they really were then

God could have given them much to make them rich.

But they didn't listen. If you visit Laodicea today, the once magnificent city is a pile of rubble stretching for acres. As I write these words, I have in front of me a small piece of marble that easily fits into a hand. I picked it up from a field of broken stones that was once Laodicea, and I keep it on my desk to remind me about the danger of hearing God's word and ignoring it, and the danger of forgetting who I really am—and what Jesus can make me.

God can only fill hands that are truly empty and he can only heal hearts that are really broken.

Workout

1. Our first close look at the Beatitudes has brought us back to basics: who we are and how God sees us. How do you see yourself? Are you dependent on God for your spiritual life or do you secretly think you can rely on your own resources? Ask God to show you the needs in your life—and learn to ask him to meet them.

2. Jesus said, 'I have come that they may have life, and have it to the full' (John 10:10). There's a sense in which that has to encompass both the highest joy *and* the deepest sorrow. Sorrow is painful, a broken heart brings pain. Have you known that real brokenness in your life over your sin? (We will never experience real forgiveness unless we have experienced real repentance.)

3. As you pray about different situations in the world around you, ask God how he feels about those things. What breaks God's heart?

Prayer

Dear Father, help me to realize that in myself I have nothing. Please forgive me for my pride in myself. Please forgive me for my hardness of heart that often stops me from really being sorry and really showing brokenness in my life. I don't want to get by on my own or pretend that my heart isn't broken. I need you to fill me and to heal me. Amen.

PS

I am nothing without you,
   I'm not ashamed to say.
But sometimes still I doubt you
   Along my way.
I am nothing without you,
   An eagle, without wings.
If I forget about you
   I lose everything.

From Paul Field, *Empty Page*, copyright © Word Music (UK) 1979.
Used by permission.

8

Meekness Is Not Weakness

Readings

Psalm 37:1–40; Matthew 5:5–6

Think through

'Blessed are the go-getters'; 'Happy are the aggressive';
'Joy to those who push their way to the front of the
queue.' These could be the Beatitudes for modern-day
Britain. Our Society seems to go out of its way to encourage a strong 'up-front' image.

'There's no way he's saying that to me and getting
away with it!'; 'What does she think I am—a doormat?';
'I don't care what you say...I'm doing it anyway!' If
we're honest, haven't we all heard ourselves saying things
like that? We applaud Sinatra when he sings 'I did it my
way' and moan when someone pinches our parking space!

In this chapter, two more jigsaw pieces of the Christian
character snap into place, but be prepared for a shock
because the kingdom values of Jesus turn our standards
upside down.

Learning who's in charge

'Blessed are the meek, for they will inherit the earth'
(Matthew 5:5).

We make a big mistake when we think the word
'meek' equals 'weak'. We wrongly associate meekness
with being wet when it is, in fact, the exact opposite. The
Greek word *praus* means gentle, humble and patient. It
means being able to keep your cool when others are
losing theirs—and there is nothing even slightly damp
about that.

It takes great self-control (or, more accurately, God-
control) to be truly meek. The whole of Psalm 37 is a
commentary on this Beatitude. Read it through carefully
and notice how Jesus seems to be echoing verse 11 of the
Psalm, which says: 'But the meek will inherit the land
and enjoy great peace.'

How can we learn to let the Holy Spirit help the fruit
of meekness to grow in our lives?

1. *It means having a true estimate of yourself*

It's possible to take courses on 'self-assertiveness', and
one exercise involves standing in front of the mirror first
thing in the morning with a fixed grin and reciting as
follows: 'Good Morning! You're a winner, you were
born a winner, you were made to win and you are going
to win. Now go out and get 'em.'

There is a Christian equivalent of this strange ritual
that some of us indulge in often, only this time the
routine runs: 'Woe is me, I'm a loser, defeated,
depressed, discouraged, single/married [delete as
appropriate]…'

In fact, I think it would be helpful if some talented
musician could set 'Woe is me' to music as a chorus!

I'm being extreme, and deliberately so. Meekness is
to do with having a realistic picture of myself and a true

understanding of the Lord Jesus Christ. Going back to the mirror routine, we should say: 'In myself I'm a loser—but in Christ I'm a winner.' Paul expresses something of this in Philippians 3:7–11.

2. It means living a God-controlled life

The word 'meekness' is sometimes used of an animal that has been broken in. Imagine a wild stallion free to run wherever it pleases. It is taken and gradually trained to accept bit and bridle and eventually saddle and rider. The horse has not been crushed, but it has been broken. You end up with controlled strength and directed energy. That is a picture of what the Lord Jesus Christ can do in your life if you give him first place.

3. It means gentleness

If you want to look at meekness in more depth, the Bible mentions two outstanding examples: Moses (Numbers 12:3) and Jesus Christ (Matthew 21:5). Study their lives, and you'll find that neither of them were weak men. They were both angry at times and faced opposition and criticism. Yet there was a gentleness of spirit that conveyed controlled strength.

Jesus is our greatest example and the Beatitudes draw for us a picture of his character, and when you look at him you certainly discover that meekness does not equal weakness.

But how do the meek 'inherit the earth'? No doubt there is a future application of this phrase in the new earth, but it also means a great deal in the here and now. The person who lives a God-centred, God-controlled life discovers the richness of living as God intended. The earth and everything in it becomes theirs in Christ—as Paul put it—'having nothing, and yet possessing everything' (2 Corinthians 6:10).

The graffiti artist got it wrong when he scrawled on the

wall: 'The meek will inherit the earth (if that's all right with the rest of you).'

Learning where you're headed

'Blessed are those who hunger and thirst for righteousness for they will be filled' (Matthew 5:6).

Food and water are essential to life. Jesus uses the words 'hunger' and 'thirst' to drive home the point that our desire for righteousness should not be a passing feeling that comes and goes, but a deep-seated sense of continuing need.

There are different ways in which we can understand this. There is a hunger in the human heart to know God. Not everyone can identify it as this, but the need is there in us all. The only way this hunger can be satisfied is when we come in repentance and faith and commit our lives to Jesus Christ.

If you are a Christian, then there should be in your life a sense of hunger to please God. That hunger gets blunted from time to time and we need to learn how to sharpen our appetites.

Another evidence that you are a child of God is a hunger to serve God. In this context of hungering and thirsting for righteousness it means caring about God's world and the people in it. That caring means sharing the good news about Jesus and it also means expressing God's concern about righteousness. God cares about injustice, poverty and oppression in every form.

John Stott expresses it so well when he writes: 'Christians are committed to hunger for righteousness and in the whole human community as something pleasing to a righteous God.'

What matters most in life to you? What are your dreams and ambitions? Where are you headed? These are vitally important questions. Jesus said: 'Seek first

[God's] kingdom and his righteousness, and all these things will be given to you as well' (Matthew 6:33).

The Beatitudes are Jesus' identikit picture of a disciple and it's all beginning to fit together. The question is: do we answer the description?

Workout

1. Meekness is one of those words that has been corrupted over the years. For most of us it conjures up a weak, pale, ineffectual, 'ever so humble' type of character. We've read in this chapter, however, that true humility and gentleness of temper are definitely not weak characteristics. How do you see yourself? As a loser? As a winner? Do you exhibit meekness in your life?

2. The Good News Bible's interpretation of Matthew 5:6 is: 'Happy are those whose greatest desire is to do what God requires; God will satisfy them fully!' Is doing God's will your 'greatest desire' in life? How sharp is your appetite to please him?

3. Now that we've covered the first half of the jigsaw, how do you match up with the picture so far?

Prayer

'Gentle Jesus, meek and mild'—I've heard that prayer so often and dismissed it when I grew out of nursery rhymes. Help me to show your gentleness, your meekness and mildness of temper—your control in my life. I really do want to do your will. Help me to want that above all else. When people meet me may they know that Jesus really lives in me. Amen.

PS

Meekness and Majesty, Manhood and Deity,
   In perfect harmony. The Man who is God.
Lord of Eternity dwells in humanity,
   Kneels in humility and washes our feet.

O what a mystery
   Meekness and majesty—
Bow down and worship
   For this is your God. This is your God.

Father's pure radiance, perfect in innocence
   Yet learns obedience to death on a cross.
Suffering to give us life, conquering through sacrifice
   And as they crucify prays 'Father forgive'.

Wisdom unsearchable, God the invisible
   Love indestructible in frailty appears.
Lord of infinity, stooping so tenderly
   Lifts our humanity to the heights of his throne.

O what a mystery
   Meekness and Majesty—
Bow down and worship
   For this is your God. This is your God.
This is your God.

Graham Kendrick, *This is your God*, copyright © Thankyou Music 1986. Used by permission.

9

Family Traits

Readings

Matthew 5:7–8; 18:15–35

Think through

It's only a tiny bundle—8lbs of pink humanity, wet, smelly and screaming. Curious onlookers begin to crowd around and give their signs of approval. A host of ridiculous comments follow, such as: 'He's got his father's nose!' 'Yes, and those are Gladys' ears all right and Uncle George's feet—there's no mistaking who he belongs to.'

People are looking for a family likeness. It's natural to do it. New parents expect it, and even enjoy it, because in finding things that are similar we are actually saying, 'You belong to the family—and it shows.'

It should also show if we belong to God's family.

As we continue our look at the Beatitudes we find two more of the jigsaw pieces of the Christian character: mercy and purity.

Learning how to forgive

'Blessed are the merciful, for they will be shown mercy' (Matthew 5:7).

There is nothing worse than being eaten up by anger. Resentment is a slow-burning fire, but it does more damage to us than to the person we feel angry towards. Jesus is saying plainly that we have to deal with other people on the basis that God deals with us—mercifully.

Just after teaching his disciples the Lord's Prayer, which contains the phrase, 'Forgive us our debts as we also have forgiven our debtors,' Jesus adds this devastating comment: 'If you do not forgive men their sins, your Father will not forgive your sins' (Matthew 6:15).

If we will not forgive, then we can't be forgiven. When truth like that begins to challenge our motives and attitudes we automatically run for the cover of our exemption clauses: 'But you don't understand what they did to me!'; 'They have never even said "sorry"!' 'If I let them get away with it now it will just happen again'; 'There's a limit to everyone's patience....'

But, no matter how hard we wriggle, truth remains truth: *'If you will not forgive you will not be forgiven.'*

1. It is mercy that comes from God

'God has poured out his love into our hearts by the Holy Spirit' (Romans 5:5). God can give you the power to forgive if you have the willingness to forgive.

One of the marks that God's grace is at work in your life is that you are grateful. Gratitude is the fruit, and grace is the root. We demonstrate that gratitude in our willingness to be merciful.

2. It is mercy from the heart

We can say outwardly that something is forgiven and

forgotten and yet inwardly we can be smouldering. Like the little girl who was repeatedly told to sit down by her father. Eventually, under threat of punishment, she sat down—only to mutter between clenched teeth, 'I may be sitting down on the outside, but on the inside I'm still standing up!'

3. It is mercy that reaches out

God's mercy reaches out to bless ungrateful people. God's forgiveness is a practical thing—removing guilt, cleaning up a life and giving a new start.

We demonstrate mercy by the way we act towards the people who least deserve it. God has shown his mercy to *us* and we have the obligation to pass that blessing on. Next time you catch yourself smouldering, read Matthew 18:15–35—quickly!

Learning how to keep clean

'Blessed are the pure in heart for they will see God' (Matthew 5:8).

'Pure' is another one of those words that has been spoilt for us. For 'pure' we read 'boring' and 'twee'. How wrong can we get!

Look at Jesus. He was pure in every way, but he could never be described as being twee or out of touch.

'Pure in heart' is a loaded phrase. Professor Tasker, in the Tyndale New Testament Commentaries, has the best definition of this phrase when he says it refers to those who are 'single minded, free from the tyranny of a divided self and who do not try to serve God and the world at the same time'.

To be pure in heart is to be single minded for God and that governs your attitudes as well as your actions. Is your heart set on going God's way and doing God's will—whatever the cost? There is nothing worse than spiritual schizophrenia where a constant internal war is being fought. Of course, we will have struggles with temptation and pressures—but beware of the 'tyranny of a divided self'.

Someone once said, 'A man is not what he thinks he is. But what he thinks—he *is*.' Purity of heart begins with the mind, as contradictory as that might sound. If you want to be transformed, try renewing your mind: 'Do not conform any longer to the pattern of this world, but be transformed by the renewing of your mind' (Romans 12:2).

Mercy and purity—two important family likenesses. Next time people start scrutinizing you to discover who you take after, make sure they know.

Workout

It's probably in the areas of mercy and purity that the majority of us fail most miserably in being like Jesus.

1. Are there people that you *can't* (or won't) forgive? As we've read, our danger and feeling of resentment can do far more damage to us than it can to the person it's directed towards! In refusing to forgive we hurt ourselves the most. The dictionary definition of 'mercy' is interesting: 'Forbearance [clemency] towards one who is in one's power.' The fact is though that in forgiving that person we become free too! Ask God to make you more aware of the mercy he's shown you. In the light of that, can you really deny someone else forgiveness?

2. How pure is your heart? Are you really determined to go God's way? In the midst of everyday pressures, is it God's will you want above all else?

Prayer

Dear Father, thank you that you understand me perfectly. Thank you that you see the struggle so often taking place inside me—wanting to do your will and wanting to show your love to others, and yet being held back by my own pride and stubbornness to really let go. Father, I do want your likeness to shine through my life. Help me, in learning more about you and growing closer to you, to become fully the person you want me to be. Thank you for your Spirit living in me. Amen.

PS

I may not be every mother's dream for her little girl.
My face may not grace the mind of everyone in the world.
But that's all right, as long as I can have one wish, I pray
When people look inside my life I want to hear them say:

> She has her Father's eyes, her Father's eyes.
> Eyes that find the good in things,
>   when good is not around.
> Eyes that find the source of help,
>   when help just can't be found.
> Eyes full of compassion,
>   seeing everything.
> Knowing what you're going through,
>   and feeling it the same.
> Just like my Father's eyes.

On that day when we will pay for all the deeds we have done,
Good and bad, they'll all be had to see by everyone.
And when you're called to stand and tell just what you saw in me
Well, more than anything I know, I want your words to be:

> She had her Father's eyes, her Father's eyes.
> Eyes that found the good in things,

when good was not around.
Eyes that found the source of help,
    when help would not be found.
Eyes full of compassion,
    seeing everything.
Knowing what you're going through,
    and feeling it the same.
Just like my Father's eyes.

From Gary Chapman, *Father's Eyes*, copyright © Paragon Music Corporation 1982.

10

Cool Christianity

Readings

Matthew 5:9–12; Hebrews 12:1–3

Think through

The blood-spattered bodies lay sprawled on the sand. Five men—young men with wives and children—had paid the ultimate price.

They had prayed for those who murdered them for six long years. The world knew nothing of the Auca Indians, a primitive, stone-age tribe that lived in the heart of Ecuador's rain forest. But the five young men knew about them, cared about them and desperately wanted to bring Jesus to them. Through the death of those men, and the prayers of God's people, there is today a church among the Aucas, and some of those who were involved in the killings have become strong leaders within it.

Peace and persecution are topics that leap off the pages of our newspapers—whether it is disputes or dissidents, punch-ups on the terraces or flare-ups in the Third World. In this final chapter on the Beatitudes,

Jesus completes the identikit picture of a disciple with the two characteristics of peace and persecution.

Learning to build bridges

'Blessed are the peacemakers, for they will be called sons of God' (Matthew 5:9).

Abraham Lincoln once said, 'Die when I may, I would like it to be said of me that I always pulled up a weed and planted a flower where I thought a flower would grow.' To make the world a better place for our being here, is not a bad goal to aim for.

Jesus said one of the ways in which we show our family likeness is in peacemaking. God is a reconciler—a bridge-builder. We demonstrate our sonship by acting like our Father. Think for a moment where peace is needed most:

1. In an individual life

The greatest need a person has is to find peace with God. Peacemaking is all to do with caring enough to share God's love in the gospel.

2. Between people

When two people fall out, the easiest thing to do is to fan the flames instead of helping to put them out. Peacemaking means doing all we can to bring people together.

3. Inside our churches

How sad it is that the one group of people on earth with more cause to be united than any other remains divided, hostile and suspicious. So often the world doubts our seriousness because it overhears our squabbles. Are you a peacemaker in the church?

4. *Within a community*

Communities all across Britain are divided. Part of the Christian task is to demonstrate that Jesus Christ can break the barriers of race, money, class and religion.

5. *Among nations*

Mankind has the weapons to destroy itself many times over. Millions starve while millions are spent to sophisticate the art of murder. More than at any other time in the world's history, the Christian church has both cause and opportunity to be peacemakers among nations.

Peacemaking starts with me in my everyday relationships. Sadly, we find it easier to burn bridges instead of building them—but if you are a child of your Father then you will want to start to reverse that process.

Learning to keep going

> Blessed are you when people insult you, persecute you and falsely say all kinds of evil against you because of me. Rejoice and be glad, because great is your reward in heaven, for in the same way they persecuted the prophets who were before you (Matthew 5:11–12).

Are you a 'cool' Christian? Are you a Christian who doesn't want it to disrupt your lifestyle too much? 'It's simply not "cool" to drag faith into everything. I mean, we need to relate to people culturally, in a way they understand. We can't ram religion down their throats, can we?'

There is nothing 'cool' about being a Christian, so you may as well stop playing the game. Hassle and hardship are part of the package. Jesus is speaking here about insults, persecution, lies and slanderous accusations. That is normal Christianity. Try setting the image of 'cool' Christianity alongside Jesus' powerful statement:

'Woe to you when all men speak well of you' (Luke 6:26).

Jesus tells his disciples to 'rejoice' when the pressure is on, not only because heaven is a place for righting injustice and receiving rewards, but also because persecution puts us in the ranks of the spiritual greats.

If you feel today a sense of privilege in your freedom (and you should), then thank God for your opportunities and use them. And never forget to pray for others in the Christian family who suffer for their faith.

Perhaps you are pressured for being a Christian in your family, at school or where you work. Then re-read this last Beatitude and thank God that you are not unusual.

Luke's version reads: 'Rejoice in that day and leap for joy' (Luke 6:23)—which could possibly be used by those desperately seeking proof texts to justify Christian aerobics! Dietrich Bonhoeffer, who died in a concentration camp in World War Two for his steadfast Christian denunciation of the Nazis, once wrote: 'Suffering, then, is the badge of true discipleship.'

It costs to be a bridge-builder, as those five young Americans discovered in the Ecuador rain forest in 1956. Read the Beatitudes through the world's eyes and you reach one conclusion: anyone who lives like that is a fool and a loser. But Christians know differently!

Jim Elliot—one of the five—wrote in his diary as a college student seven years before being asked to lay his life on the line for what he believed: 'He is no fool who gives what he cannot keep to gain what he cannot lose....'

Workout

1. The Jewish people have a lovely way of greeting each other. They say 'Shalom'. This word basically means

'peace', but it goes deeper than that, meaning 'completeness', 'soundness', 'well-being'. (That indicates just how much of a positive force peacemakers can have!)

Look at the various areas where peace is most needed at the moment: in an individual life; between two people you know; inside your church; within your community; among nations of the world. Make a note of one example from each category and begin to pray specifically for God's peace in those situations. (Are you willing for God to use *you* as a maker of peace in some of those situations?)

2. How do you react when people malign you and insult you for being a Christian? One Christian, when being cold-shouldered in a school staff room joked, 'I thought the persecution of Christians went out with the Romans!'

Sadly, that's not true. The most subtle attacks are the ones that seem to hurt most—a caustic aside made by a friend is probably the most common and most painful 'persecution' most of us have to cope with. Learn to share these experiences with Christian friends, don't allow the hurt to grow inside you by thinking that you're the only one ever to go through this ordeal...and learn to tell God about it too. Thank him that you are not alone and that the people around you have actually noticed you are a Christian. God may have put you in that situation for a very special purpose.

Prayer

Dear Father, reading about Christians who have given their lives for what they believe, and hearing about Christians who experience such hardship simply for following you, makes me realize how shallow my commitment to you often is. Help me to be a 'hot' Christian, with a love for you and a real commitment to see your will done on earth. Amen.

PS

Therefore, since we are surrounded by such a great cloud of witnesses, let us throw off everything that hinders and the sin that so easily entangles, and let us run with perseverance the race marked out for us. Let us fix our eyes on Jesus, the author and perfector of our faith, who for the joy set before him endured the cross, scorning its shame, and sat down at the right hand of the throne of God. Consider him who endured such opposition from sinful men, so that you will not grow weary and lose heart (Hebrews 12:1–3).

SECTION 3

Gifts for Growing

I I

Who, Me?

Readings

Exodus 3:1—4:17; John 6:5–13

Think through

Have you ever caught yourself—perhaps in the middle of a church service—thinking that you're nothing more than a useless blob?

If the answer is 'yes', then join the club. There are quite a few of us!

It usually happens when some multi-talented super-Christian is sharing their gripping testimony, before singing a track from their latest album, and then launching into a detailed exposition of 'Badgerskins in the Temple' from Leviticus. Sometimes—without meaning to—gifted Christians can make us feel very useless. If we are not careful, it doesn't take much for that to become a negative, faith-destroying force in our lives. It gives rise to jealousy and cuts us off from the flow of God's blessing. I believe it is a subtle part of Satan's strategy. He loves to make Christians feel useless, doubt God's power and get eaten away by tensions towards other believers.

The truth (which the devil cannot stand) is that God can actually use *you*. More than that, God *wants* to use you. Yes, *you*, that complex bundle of flesh and fear with all your doubts and questions. With Jesus Christ you are unstoppable.

I think of a friend of mine who today is leading a growing church—a man whose life has touched and blessed many people. He used to sell paraffin door to door, and in one of the houses he called at on his rounds there lived an elderly Christian lady. The generation and culture gaps between them were unspannable. He knew nothing of the world of hymns, prayers and Bible studies, and she knew nothing of the world of night clubs, wild parties and the drugs scene. But she believed God could use her. She began to pray for the 'Esso Blue man' and asked him in for a cup of tea when he was on his rounds. God gave her remarkable openings to share her love for Jesus, and, against all the odds, he ended up kneeling in her living room one afternoon, and accepting Christ into his life.

God's preconditions

When we look at the Bible we discover that God seems able to use anyone, no matter what colour, sex, education or upbringing. God is quite capable of using a small child, or on one occasion even an ass, to deliver his message! But there are some basic conditions that God lays down and you can trace them for yourself in the lives of men and women whom God has used.

1. Obedience

We've got to be willing to do as we're told. Obedience in small things is usually a good indication of whether we will be obedient in larger things.

2. Faith

God often calls us to take risks. If you are going to be used by God you will have to learn early on the difference between faith and presumption; spiritual vision and recklessness. But be prepared to step out for God, because faith is a risky business.

3. Willingness

It obviously begins with a willingness to be used by God, but it needs to go deeper than that. A willingness to learn is essential if we are going to be effective in serving God. We will soon discover that we don't have all the answers, and mistakes will (often) be made. We need to be both big enough and small enough to learn. Also, we need a *willingness to take direction* from others. Until we learn how to work under authority it is not much use our being entrusted with authority.

A friend of mine spoke at my wedding, applying the verse: 'Jesus took a donkey and sat upon it,' to me! I forgave him years ago, when I began to see that was exactly what God had to do in my life.

Things that hold us back

'But what about . . .' is often the response we give to the challenge that God can use us. Although we may believe that it is our own ability we are doubting, what we are really doing is expressing doubt in God's ability. After all, if he can use *anyone*, what's the problem with him using us?

Take Moses as an example. You can read about his call in Exodus 3:1—4:17. God is absolutely clear in his instructions; he wants to use Moses as his spokesman to Pharaoh. But instead of leaping up in super-spiritual obedience, Moses expresses some real doubts about the whole business. No fewer than five times he raises his objections:

* Who am I that I should get involved? (Exodus 3:11)

* What happens if they ask 'who sent you'? (Exodus 3:13)

* What if they don't believe me? (Exodus 4:1)

* I'm not good enough (Exodus 4:10)

* Please send someone else! (Exodus 4:13)

Sounds familiar, doesn't it? But Moses *did* go, even though he was a reluctant hero. God had answers for every objection he raised. In fact, those answers showed them up for what they really were—excuses for not getting involved.

The little lad with his packed lunch made everyone laugh. How on earth could a few rolls feed this huge crowd? But Jesus took what the little boy handed him, offered it to his Father for blessing, broke the rolls and passed the packed lunch out to a hungry crowd. It was nothing to start with, but when Jesus got hold of it there was enough for a multitude.

One little boy that day gave grown men a lesson in Christian discipleship. If you offer all you have in obedience and faith, with a willing heart, not only will God use you, but you'll also see the blessing touch other lives too.

So be encouraged, on days when you feel nothing more than a fish sandwich . . . God can use you too.

Workout

1. Have you ever stopped to think about the wonder that God would want to use *you*? God, in his grace, has

chosen to use us as his instruments here on earth. Are you willing to be used by God?

2. When God calls he is faithful. As we step out in obedience to his call in our lives, so he will meet our needs. There are numerous books about Christians who have stepped out to serve God 'against all odds' (humanly) and have found him to be completely faithful. Perhaps God isn't calling you to make a major step like going to the other side of the world. It may be that he wants to use you to visit people in hospital, or help with the church cleaning, or teach in Sunday School, or...the possibilities are endless! Are you willing to be used by God in whatever way *he* chooses?

3. There's no need to feel jealous of others either. God simply asks you to be obedient to what he says to *you*—not to get bogged down by a list of things which he hasn't called you to do anyway.

Learn to thank God that he *wants* to use you in a special and unique way. Learn to hear his voice and obey him.

Prayer

Dear Father, I ask your forgiveness for the many times I've refused to believe that you can use me (or, in fact, that you should want to use me). Please forgive me for comparing myself with others and for feeling jealous that you've chosen to use them in a certain way. Help me to hear what you're saying to *me* and to be willing to respond in obedience, trusting you to take care of the consequences. Thank you, Father. Amen.

PS

O Thou who camest from above
    The pure celestial fire to impart,
Kindle a flame of sacred love
    On the mean altar of my heart!

There let it for Thy glory burn
    With inextinguishable blaze;
And trembling to its source return,
    In humble love and fervent praise.

Jesus, confirm my heart's desire
    To work, and speak, and think for Thee;
Still let me guard the holy fire,
    And stir up Thy gift in me.

Ready for all Thy perfect will,
    My acts of faith and love repeat,
Till death Thy endless mercies seal,
    And make the sacrifice complete.

Charles Wesley

12

Discovering Your Gift—1

Readings

Romans 12:3–8; 1 Corinthians 12:1–31; Ephesians 4:11–13; 1 Peter 4:10–11

Think through

'Spiritual gifts? Well, as far as I'm concerned they are not for today—all that type of thing was needed by the early church because they didn't have complete Bibles.'

'Spiritual gifts? That's a dangerous subject. The sort of thing that divides churches. I knew a man once who spoke in tongues and his marriage broke up....'

'Spiritual gifts? Fantastic! Our pastor is really into miracles at the moment. He told me about a church in the USA where they hand live snakes around during the morning meeting, and the congregation are so spiritual they never get hurt!'

Three sad, but typical responses to an issue that is vitally important for the church if we are going to effectively serve God in today's world.

I find that there are three major problems worldwide on the question of spiritual gifts:

* Ignorance: We are simply unclear or, worse still, un-
  taught about what spiritual gifts are and how they
  should be used.

* Fear: Spiritual gifts do not divide churches. Unloving,
  immature Christians do!

* Imbalance: One of the greatest traps Christians fall
  into is extremism. The issue of spiritual gifts is not
  without its own peculiar minefields. That is why we
  need to have a biblical understanding coupled with
  humble hearts and loving leadership if we are going to
  receive and use all that God has for us.

Ignorance, fear and imbalance are not new problems
when it comes to spiritual gifts. Paul realized that the
young church in Corinth was facing these types of
problems. That is why he wrote to them saying: 'Now
about spiritual gifts, brothers, I do not want you to be
ignorant' (1 Corinthians 12:1).

We need a biblical framework too. Not only to understand what we are talking about, but also to learn how to
use the gifts the Lord Jesus Christ gives to his body, the
church. So let's begin by asking some basic questions:

What are spiritual gifts?

The word for 'spiritual gift' is the Greek word *charisma*
which means 'a gift of God's grace'. It comes from the
word *charis* which is a beautiful, biblical word meaning
'grace'. Spiritual gifts are God's love gifts to his church.
James reminds us that 'every good and perfect gift is
from above, coming down from the Father of the
heavenly lights' (James 1:17). That is why we need to be
so careful how we speak about spiritual gifts. They are
good and perfect and come from God himself!

There are four major passages on spiritual gifts and

ministries in the New Testament (listed above). In those passages different lists of gifts appear, but nowhere is it suggested that these are complete lists. Elsewhere in the New Testament, celibacy and marriage are referred to as charismatic-spiritual gifts; leadership, forgiveness, giving and fellowship are described in the same way. Some gifts are obviously supernatural but others seem to be natural gifts that are given back to God and used for his glory. Paul sums it up well by telling the Corinthian Christians:

> There are different kinds of gifts, but the same Spirit. There are different kinds of service, but the same Lord. There are different kinds of working, but the same God works all of them in all men (1 Corinthians 12:4–6).

So beware of getting squeezed into anyone else's mould as to what are the most important gifts—we need all that we can get if we are going to serve God effectively in the world in which he has placed us. Tongues, prophecy and gifts of healing are important—but so are hospitality, forgiveness and faith!

Where do they come from?

God is the giver, by the Holy Spirit. No one else can give you a spiritual gift, and years of Christian service or even theological training are not a means of gaining those gifts. God gives them—and he is the One we need to ask for them. The New Testament strongly suggests that every Christian has at least one spiritual gift, and we are positively encouraged to ask God for more. We are told: 'Each one should use whatever gift he has received to serve others, faithfully administering God's grace in its various forms' (1 Peter 4:10).

Why are they given?

A friend of mine related how his young daughter had gone into his tool shed and picked up a chisel, badly gashing her hand. A trip to the hospital and several stitches later, he tried to explain to her the danger of using a tool as a toy. I will never forget his point. God has given his gifts as *tools* to be used, not *toys* to be played with. It is when we 'play around' with spiritual gifts that we cut and hurt the body of Christ.

God has not given his gifts to make us spiritual exhibitionists, dazzling the world with our skills and abilities. The church is not meant to be in the entertainment business but engaged in the task of kingdom-building.

If we are going to do God's work, we need to use the gifts he gives to us with a great sense of responsibility which flows from an understanding of our accountability both to God and to his children.

It is of great significance that Paul, in the middle of teaching the church at Corinth, writes about the body of Christ. We are all different parts with different functions. No one is more important than anyone else. Use the gift that God has given you, not for selfish reasons, but for the good of the body of Christ.

How are they to be used?

The four New Testament passages that I mentioned earlier give us answers to this all-important question:

As a faithful servant of others

They are not for self-service, but for serving others (1 Peter 4:10).

With faith and obedience

If God has given you gifts use them. Don't worry about

your inadequacy or inexperience. Use what you have received (Romans 12:6).

With a sense of purpose

Ephesians 4:10ff refers to ministry gifts such as apostle, prophet, evangelist, pastor and teacher. But notice why these gifts are given: 'To prepare God's people for works of service.' Gifts are given to equip others with God's gifts, and to train them in how to use them.

In the context of the body of Christ

The New Testament has no room for lone rangers and neither should we. Our tasks and gifts must always be seen in the light of the gifts and tasks others have too. Like instruments in an orchestra, what we play may sound different from everyone else, but as we follow the conductor together we discover harmony (1 Corinthians 12:12ff).

In the next chapter we are going to cover a few more basic questions before looking at how you can discover your spiritual gift and begin serving God in today's world.

Workout

1. Read through the passages that have been mentioned (Romans 12:3–8; 1 Corinthians 12:1–31; Ephesians 4:11–13; 1 Peter 4:10–11) and list the various spiritual gifts that are found there.

2. With the aid of a good concordance, discover how many things are described as *charisma* (spiritual gifts) in the New Testament.

3. David Watson's book *Discipleship* (Hodder and Stoughton) has a challenging and useful chapter on this subject entitled 'Life in the Spirit'.

Prayer

Dear Father, thank you for the variety of spiritual gifts that you have given to your children and that those gifts are available to us now. Thank you for the potential in your church if each one of us really exercised the gifts that you have given. Thank you for the potential in my life if I am faithful in using the gift (or gifts) you have given me. Amen.

PS

For by the grace given me I say to every one of you: Do not think of yourself more highly than you ought, but rather think of yourself with sober judgment, in accordance with the measure of faith God has given you. Just as each of us has one body with many members, and these members do not all have the same function, so in Christ we who are many form one body, and each member belongs to all the others. We have different gifts according to the grace given us (Romans 12:3–6).

13

Discovering Your Gift—2

Reading

1 Corinthians 12–14

Think through

Yesterday afternoon, at around 3.30, World War Three hit our living room. One of my sons was holding a birthday party to celebrate five years of existence. Do you realize how much noise a room full of children can make without really trying?

One thing gripped me. Each friend had brought a small gift for the birthday boy, and with a complete lack of inhibition the wrappers were greedily ripped off the presents. Everyone was fighting to get a look and, more than anything, a first 'try' of the gift.

How would you react if, when you gave a present to a friend, they responded with a shrug of the shoulders, a suspicious look or, worse still, a flat no to receiving your gift? I wonder how God feels when, faced with the needs of a waiting world, he finds his children debating over the tools for the job. God gives gifts in order that we can do his work in his way.

In the last chapter we began to look at some of the basic questions that are raised about spiritual gifts: what are spiritual gifts? Where do they come from? Why are they given? How are they to be used? Here are some other questions that we need to face:

When is a natural gift a spiritual gift?

We sometimes hear a person described as a 'born leader' or a 'gifted musician'. Possibly you can recognize areas in your own life where you have a real gift or natural ability—music, art, friendship-making, practical or administrative skills—the list is endless. But what makes a natural gift a spiritual gift (if such a thing can happen)? This is a very important question and if we fail to get it right it leads to all sorts of complications.

From the New Testament I find four things need to happen for a natural gift to be used supernaturally—in other words, taken up and used by God.

1. *The gift must be given back to God.* (See Romans 12:1—'living sacrifice' means offering all that I am and have back to God, and that includes skills and abilities.)

2. *The gift must be used trusting in God's power and not my own talent.* (See John 15:5—'I am the vine; you are the branches. If a man remains in me and I in him, he will bear much fruit; apart from me you can do nothing.')

3. *A natural gift can be seen as a spiritual gift when it is used for God's glory and not simply to boost my ego.* (Colossians 3:17—'And whatever you do, whether in word or deed, do it all in the name of the Lord Jesus, giving thanks to God the Father through him.')

4. *The gift must be given back to God for him to use*—to feed and encourage his church and to share his love in the world. (1 Peter 4:10—'Each one should use whatever gift he has received to serve others, faithfully administering God's grace in its various forms.')

Sadly, these are lessons that we are sometimes slow to learn as Christians, and our local church or young people's fellowship can be run like an extension of the Civil Service. Everything is organized efficiently, but somehow there is an aching absence of the presence of God. I am not saying that good management is not needed in the church, simply that we sometimes manage so well that the Holy Spirit has no room to move.

I remember preaching overseas a few years ago and was told that on a particular evening the message would be interpreted by a man who was a skilled linguist holding a government post. He was used to translating at high level military conferences and diplomatic summits. Sometimes preaching through translation can be a depressing business, so I felt more than glad that on this rare occasion I would be in the hands of an expert. The evening was a disaster. I discovered later that the man was not a committed Christian. Skilful though he was, that evening in the pulpit he was lost. I learned an important lesson: you can't do God's work with men's methods.

Who controls a spiritual gift?

This is a question some of us have in the back of our minds often in relation to gifts such as tongues and prophecy. We have an inbuilt resistance to being taken over by an unknown force and made to perform in a trance-like state. But God is not in the business of making tailors' dummies do robotics. You are a person, and the Holy Spirit makes you more of a person (in the sense of becoming whole), not a mindless machine.

Look at 1 Corinthians 14:32–33: 'The spirits of prophets are subject to the control of prophets. For God is not a God of disorder but of peace.'

As we surrender our lives to the Holy Spirit we

discover that we don't lose control; instead we find that part of his fruit is self-control. Paul is telling the Corinthian church that Christian worship is not meant to be like an out-of-control farmyard—any more than it is meant to be like a mortuary!

So don't let fear keep you back from the good things God wants to give you.

Am I allowed to ask God for spiritual gifts?

Yes, in fact we are specifically told to: 'Eagerly desire the greater gifts' (1 Corinthians 12:31). 'Follow the way of love and eagerly desire spiritual gifts, especially the gift of prophecy' (1 Corinthians 14:1).

The word used for 'eagerly desire' could also be translated 'covet'. There is a sense in which we are allowed a holy jealousy when it comes to seeking God for his gifts. We don't have because we don't ask, and God makes it clear that we are to seek him with open hands and hungry hearts for all that he wants to give us. But be clear about your motives. God is not concerned with building you into a superstar but developing you into a servant.

How can I discover my spiritual gift?

I have set out some guidelines below to help you, and over the next three chapters we will be looking at some of the practical ways in which we can move out in serving God.

Be *open* for all that God has for you; be *ready* to take a deep look into your Bible; be *willing* to spend time seeking God; be *available* for him to use you at any time, night or day, and be *teachable* (we all get it wrong sometimes, but it is important to learn how to learn from mistakes, especially when that involves being corrected by others). Go forward with this sort of attitude and you will go far with God.

Workout

1. Make an honest assessment of yourself. Do you have natural ability or special skills? Are there certain things that God has allowed to happen in your life? What do you *enjoy* doing most as a Christian? (That is not such an unspiritual question as it may sound!)

2. Ask a close and honest Christian friend to assess you.

3. Ask a Christian leader (pastor, elder, YPF leader, etc.) who knows you well to assess your gifts and abilities.

4. Compare the three lists! (It could mean 'Return to Go and don't collect £200'!) Are there some things that appear on each list?

5. Ask God for specific gifts; take him up on his word.

6. If you believe God has given you a specific gift, look for ways in which you can exercise and develop it in serving others. Christian Union, youth group, church, using your summer holidays to serve God—just some of the ways you can explore. Move out in faith with what God has given you.

7. Never forget you are a *servant*. 'It's not a wise use of my gifts' can sound heavily super-spiritual, when it's really an excuse for 'go find someone else to give out your lousy Guest Service invitations'! Get your hands dirty for God—don't turn down menial jobs.

8. Seek to reproduce your gift/ministry in others. Don't be selfish but be constantly looking for ways to build up others.

9. The Christian life is dynamic not static. As you grow, some gifts may lessen and others be given.

10. Never forget 1 Corinthians 13. In the middle of two helpful chapters of truth God has sandwiched a

timely reminder. Without love, we are nothing. 'Follow the way of love *and* eagerly desire spiritual gifts,' is a perfect balance.

Prayer

Thank you, dear Father, that you love to give good gifts to your children. Help me to be willing to ask for gifts and then to be willing to receive them. Fill me again with your Holy Spirit that I may serve you in your power, not my own, always eager to let your love shine through me to others. Amen.

PS

Teach me to be a prophet,
Listen to what you say.
Tomorrow give me wisdom
From what I learn today.
Teach me to be a little child
And take the simple way.
Pride makes me complicate
And talk when I should pray.

I want to learn to worship you,
Give you all your worth,
Leave the things that I desire
And only learn to serve.
Teach me to be a servant,
To go beyond the mile.
Give me the grace I need
To face the battles and the trials.

Teach me to be a healer,
Feel the need around me.
Take away this heart of stone,
Let your love surround me.
Teach me to be a lover,

Not afraid to feel.
Give me the gift of giving love
And make the giving real.

Phil Potter and Michael Dunn, *Teach Me*, copyright © Thankyou
Music 1980. Used by permission.

14

Dirty Hands

Reading

Romans 12:1–2

Think through

When you're fifteen, with nothing to do and no one to do it with, life can be very boring. But if you decide to use the time for God, it can turn out to be quite an investment.

Take a typical teenager on a long, lazy Saturday after-noon. He hadn't been in the best of health and it had left him out of things a bit. By today's standards, in your average youth group, he'd definitely have been voted a bit wimpish. But God never looks at people in the same way we do (which is just as well really!). This guy decided to spend some time alone with God. He was only a few months old as a Christian, and things were still a bit new to him. Alone in his room that afternoon something special happened which affected the whole course of his life. Here's his own version of what happened:

I besought Him [God] to give me some work to do for Him, as an outlet for love and gratitude; some self-denying service, no matter what it might be, however trying or trivial; something with which He would be pleased, and that I might do for Him who had done so much for me...

The presence of God became unutterably real and blessed; and though but a child under sixteen, I remember stretching myself on the ground and lying there silent before Him with unspeakable awe and unspeakable joy.

The language may be from the last century, but it communicates something deep that happened the day God began to open up the vast land of China to the young Hudson Taylor. Read his thrilling life story and you will find that by the end of his life he had a team of 650 dedicated workers in all parts of China confronting spiritism and the occult head on, and seeing the kingdom of God extend into the lives of people who had never heard the gospel before. Hudson Taylor could trace it all back to that afternoon when he spent time alone with God.

Perhaps the most important part of discovering that God has given you a spiritual gift is learning to use it! A friend of mine who is a doctor was once faced with a patient who was a dedicated jogger. He wanted to get over his bout of flu quickly in order to pound the streets once more. 'You see,' he explained to the GP, 'I'm training.'

'What for?' my friend asked, only to be met by a puzzled look and silence!

It is possible to become dependent on conferences and concerts, drifting from event to event looking for another spiritual 'high', while all the time missing out on the real world.

The truth is, God wants you to have a clean heart, but dirty hands. He wants you to be involved in his world and his church. He does not want his people to be pew warmers but an army of world-shakers.

I want to focus on one verse that sets us all in that direction:

> Therefore, I urge you, brothers, in view of God's mercy, to offer your bodies as living sacrifices, holy and pleasing to God—which is your spiritual worship (Romans 12:1).

As one Christian graffiti artist so eloquently put it: 'The only trouble with a living sacrifice is that it keeps crawling off the altar!' Dead sacrifices never cause that problem—they can't move. But as you and I well know, offering our lives to Jesus involves grim determination and a daily act of obedience.

This is all to do with using your spiritual gift—a living sacrifice means offering all that you are and have to God for him to use. In the first couple of verses of Romans 12 we discover four important reasons why we need to make our lives a daily offering:

> Therefore, I urge you, brothers, in view of God's mercy, to offer your bodies as living sacrifices, holy and pleasing to God—which is your spiritual worship. Do not conform any longer to the pattern of this world, but be transformed by the renewing of your mind. Then you will be able to test and approve what God's will is—his good, pleasing and perfect will (Romans 12:1–2).

1. It pleases God

To offer ourselves as living sacrifices is the only response we can truly make in the light of God's mercy and love towards us. In the words of another great missionary pioneer, C. T. Studd: 'If Jesus Christ be God and died for me, then no sacrifice can be too great for me to make for him.'

2. It is spiritual worship

Words come easy. It is a cliché, but it is true that actions speak louder than words. We show God how much we think of him, not only in what we sing and pray on Sunday but the way we act on Monday.

3. It leads to change

The world is always demanding that we cut ourselves out according to its pattern. But God's plan is that instead of being *conformed* we should be *transformed* by renewed thinking. A changed mind leads to a changed life, and being a living sacrifice involves a day-by-day surrendering of our minds (ambitions, attitudes, thought patterns, values) to the transforming power of God. That does not mean we end up becoming brainless robots—rather that we learn what it means to be truly human.

4. It leads us forward in God's will

Daily obedience moves us on in God's plan for our lives. His will is always 'good, pleasing and perfect', and the way to test it out is to obey him!

Have you discovered your spiritual gift? If so, are you using what God has entrusted to you? I want to suggest some ways forward:

* *Start where you are.* Look for opportunities to exercise and develop your gift in your local church, youth group, Christian Union or house group. Forget great dreams of serving God somewhere else until you're willing to start where you are.

* *Get alongside someone who can help you.* Whatever you believe God is calling you into—preaching, teaching, administrative tasks or a music ministry—find someone who is exercising that sort of gift. If you believe God

wants you involved in evangelism, find someone who is being used as an evangelist and learn all you can from him—mistakes as well!

* *Learn to be faithful in small things.* Even if God leads you into a small, unglamorous job, go for it with all you've got! The way forward is to be faithful and committed to what God asks you to do.

> His master replied, 'Well done, good and faithful servant! You have been faithful with a few things; I will put you in charge of many things' (Matthew 25:21).

* *Learn to be a servant.* That is not easy! Sometimes we can get a complex about 'fulfilling *our* ministry'. We look upon certain tasks as being beneath us. But Jesus is more concerned that we learn to be effective servants, and we'll discover that instead of cramping our gifts, this actually develops them.

* *Invest time—don't waste it!* Learn to use the spare hours for God. How about using your holiday time to be involved in some of the incredible opportunities for serving God in this country and overseas? Beach missions, Tell a Tourist, European Witness Teams—the opportunities are everywhere!

I opened a letter at the breakfast table this morning that puts all of this into context. It was from a young lady who, after qualifying as a nurse decided that she wanted to invest time for God. She was writing from Africa, from a very different culture. A lot of things are tough, but God is using her. One word leapt from every line of the letter as I read it: *growth*. She is moving forward in God's purpose for her life. Are you?

Workout

1. Are you getting your hands dirty for God? Are you willing to spend time with God asking him to show you what he wants you to do for him?

2. God also gives us commonsense! Are there opportunities around *now* for you to exercise and develop the gift that God has given you?

3. Look through the other practical guidelines listed: find someone who can help you; learn to be faithful in small things; learn to be a servant; don't waste time! How can you apply these things to your life now?

Prayer

Father, my prayer is that you will lead me on in your purpose for my life. I want to know growth and development in my relationship with you. I want to give myself again to you as a living sacrifice—for you to use in your way, for your glory. Amen.

PS

I looked upon my life
And realised at last
Within myself
There's nothing I can do.
And yet here I stand
To offer all I am
And give myself
Completely, Lord, to you.

Take my life, a living sacrifice
Knowing it's the least that I can do.
Make my life a living sacrifice
Holy and acceptable to you.

I cannot be content
Until I reach that place.
How little
I have given up to you.
Lord, break down my will
Make my desires your own,
I long to give
My everything to you.

Take my life, a living sacrifice
Knowing it's the least that I can do.
Make my life a living sacrifice
Holy and acceptable to you.

Dwight Liles, *Living Sacrifice*, copyright © Kenwood Music 1980. Used by permission.

15

Extravagant Serving

Reading

John 12:1–7

Think through

Bernard C. Welch was serving a staggering 143-year sentence for robbery and murder in a maximum security jail in Chicago. He had been transferred to that particular jail to advise prison officials on possible escape routes and to give an assessment on the security of the place. While compiling his report, he took the chance to demonstrate his findings by escaping through a window using 75-feet of cable from a floor polisher, taking with him his trusty assistant—a fellow con.

A lot of egg was left on a lot of important faces! As I read the newspaper report of the event, a quote from a court official talking about Welch caught my eye: 'He is the most articulate, brightest, most capable criminal I've ever known.' What a waste—a thinking mind and such creative energy given over totally to crime.

Just a few days after reading that piece I found myself

gazing around in a church service, instead of singing the hymns, at dozens of lives full of potential, and wondering....

How can our potential be used by God to the full? We have been looking at spiritual gifts—what they are, where they come from and how they are to be used. We have also seen how God wants the whole of us—the living sacrifice of our lives—not just bits and pieces such as a few odd hours each week. But how can the potential in a life given to God and equipped by his Spirit be realized to the full?

There is a helpful passage in the Bible which provides some positive and negative examples about serving God. John 12:1–7 paints the scene of Jesus in a home in the town of Bethany, a few miles from Jerusalem. Not long before, Jesus had raised Lazarus from the dead at Bethany, so it is hardly surprising that Lazarus, Martha and Mary should throw a party in his honour.

But the two characters who stand out at the party, at least for John, are Mary and Judas.

Mary took a pint of pure nard (which was an expensive perfume) and poured it over Jesus' feet, wiping them with her hair. This is an act which to twentieth-century western minds seems strange in the extreme. And even to those present in the room it was regarded as most definitely 'over the top'. But Jesus commends Mary's action and raises no objection to what she did. '"Leave her alone," Jesus replied. "It was meant that she should save this perfume for the day of my burial"' (verse 7).

Judas was critical—the perfume worked out at almost a year's wages for an ordinary workman—and it seemed to him like extravagance gone mad.

Mary and Judas provide interesting and important contrasts about realizing our potential as servants.

Mary—a lesson about serving the right way

In case we are tempted to think that breaking open an expensive jar of perfume has little to do with real service for God, it is worth looking at the motives which moved Mary to action.

What she did came from a heart of love

Mary had many reasons to be grateful to Jesus. He had touched her life, raised her brother from the dead and left an indelible mark on her family. Whatever God does is good, and Mary, in a selfless way, was expressing her thanks. Love makes you do crazy and extravagant things. If you have tasted grace it makes you grateful and her actions were a demonstration of that.

This is where real service begins. Check your motives carefully and constantly. If you are always wanting to be recognized and thanked for what you are doing it is a giveaway sign that the motive for true service has become clouded.

What she did was costly

The perfume was expensive, and, from what we can tell, Mary was not a wealthy woman. Real service for God can be heart-aching, back-breaking stuff. Forget glamour and congratulations. Are you willing for self-sacrifice? Perhaps God has called you to be involved in a youth club with a hundred uninterested yobs, or teaching a Bible class where you feel as if banging your head against a brick wall would be easier work, or doing street work with the rain dripping down the back of your neck. Wherever you serve and whatever you do, be prepared to give *extravagantly*.

What she did laid her open to criticism

Let's face it, we all want to be popular. No one enjoys

being misunderstood and criticized. Mary's gesture left her open to both of these things. But the person who mattered most was Jesus. It was his approval that counted.

Here is another lesson about true servanthood. The way we react to criticism shows up our motives. Christians are not in the Academy Awards business. It's God's approval that counts.

What she did made a lasting impression

John—writing years later—can remember how 'the house was filled with the fragrance of the perfume' (John 12:3). Centuries later the scent lingers on: 'I tell you the truth, wherever this gospel is preached throughout the world, what she has done will also be told, in memory of her' (Matthew 26:13).

Remember the advert on TV with the guy who nearly breaks his neck crossing roads and running up flights of stairs to give the lady with the powerful perfume a bunch of flowers? Why? Because she made an impression.

Serve God with sacrifice and not only will others notice, but their lives will be touched. For the sake of your own growth God does not always let you know how many are affected, but trust him, and he will give you just the right amount of encouragement to keep you going and the right amount of knocks to keep you humble.

Judas—a warning about serving the wrong way

Just as Mary's story is an example of serving well, the story of Judas is quite the opposite.

His service was right outwardly but wrong inwardly

A grand-sounding title and an important position don't make a servant of God. Judas was identified as one of the twelve disciples and he was entrusted to be the treasurer of the group, but those 'outward' things did not mean that there was a deep inner love for God.

He appeared to be serving God when he was really serving himself

Verse 6 tells that Judas was a thief, and the money entrusted to his safe-keeping would often be taken for his own use. But serving yourself does not only mean stealing. Feeding your own ego, bolstering up inadequacies or building a personal power base can all betray a self-service motive behind a God-service façade.

He looked for good reasons for thinking bad things

Judas felt he had good reason for objecting to Mary's extravagance (verse 5). What about the poor (social conscience)? What about the cost (good stewardship)? They sound like very spiritual questions. But Judas did not care about the poor, only about himself.

It is very easy to become critical of others, especially when their commitment to Christ shows up our deficiencies and challenges us. But the danger of criticism leading to cynicism is always present. There's something healthy about the zeal of another Christian making you want to run faster. But watch out when you are tempted to trip them up in order to overtake them in the race.

His wrong attitudes eventually led to wrong actions

The life story of Judas is a sad one. How could someone who appeared so close to Jesus end up in such a mess? There is not the space to go into the complex issues here and now, but there is an important point that we must not miss. Wrong attitudes lead to wrong actions. That is why we need to keep in close touch with God.

All of us need the compass re-setting at regular

intervals, in order to get back on track. Only the Holy Spirit can do the work that is needed of sifting motives and changing attitudes. Watch out for the creeping disease of criticism and deal with it quickly.

The story of Mary and Judas gives us good things to follow and bad things to avoid in exercising gifts for God.

Jim Graham told a packed Spring Harvest once that self-examination is a healthy exercise for all engaged in doing something for God. He gave some penetrating questions that we need to ask ourselves:

* What am I doing?

* Why am I doing it?

* Who am I doing it for?

* How am I doing it?

Stick those questions on your bathroom mirror, in the front of your Bible or over the TV screen—anything to keep them in front of you. The answers are important if you want to see the powerful release of the potential God has placed within you.

Workout

1. How are you serving God? What motivates you? Look through the characteristics of Mary's service again. It came from a heart of love, it was selfless, it was costly, it left her open to criticism and it was of lasting value. Ask God to make those qualities hallmarks of your service for him.

2. So often we can start well, but end up with wrong attitudes. There are numerous individuals, small groups, churches, even denominations, through the history of the Christian church that have started well but have lost

their way in serving God. Don't allow wrong attitudes to grow in your life. Keep close to God and be ready to let the Holy Spirit sift your motives and change your attitudes.

Prayer

Thank you, Father, for the potential of a life given in serving you. Thank you too that you understand the potential in my life to do good or evil and that my motives can so easily be swayed. I want to serve you and I want my motives to be pure—please keep me close to yourself and keep me clean. Please show me now if there are any wrong attitudes or selfish motives that are spoiling my service for you. Thank you, Father. Amen.

PS

> Search me, O God, and know my heart;
>   test me and know my anxious thoughts.
> See if there is any offensive way in me,
>   and lead me in the way everlasting.
>
> (Psalm 139:23–24)

16

Faith—Don't Leave Home Without It!

Readings

Matthew 14:22–33; Hebrews 11:1–40

Think through

'If you do before you get it what you would do if you had it—then you've got it!' I've never forgotten that definition of faith, even though I can't for the life of me remember what the sermon was about! The preacher was giving the congregation an easy-to-remember slogan about faith and, despite several years of mental gymnastics at Bible College (where things simple yet profound can die the death of a thousand theological definitions), it has stuck with me.

Probably the most helpful thing about that saying is the way that faith is seen as something active, something you do. Too often faith is seen as sitting back and doing nothing and, although there is such a thing as the 'rest of faith', it is not helpful to imagine that the only way to tackle problems in the Christian life is with a deckchair and a pair of sunglasses!

Faith means believing God. Without it we cannot

please him, let alone begin to serve him effectively.

One of the most helpful examples of faith in action is seen in Peter's experience of walking on the water to Jesus (Matthew 14:22–33). If you are involved in serving God and if you want his best in your life, then make sure you pick up the three important elements of faith in Peter's story.

Leaving behind

Faith often calls us to leave behind the security of things in which we trust. Peter and the other disciples were in a boat on the Sea of Galilee on a choppy night when suddenly Jesus appeared, walking on the water. Matthew tells us, 'They were terrified. "It's a ghost," they said and cried out in fear' (verse 26). Jesus calmed them with the reassurance that they were not seeing things. It really was him, exercising his rightful authority over nature.

Peter, never backward at coming forward, makes an amazing statement: 'Lord, if it's you...tell me to come to you on the water' (verse 28). The others may have been convinced that Peter was off his head, but he was quite clear about what he was saying. If it was Jesus, then Peter could walk on the water too.

The implications were enormous; getting out of a reliable boat on a blustery night could mean getting wet (at best) or getting drowned (at worst). Peter was demonstrating his faith in Jesus and his ability to keep him safe, by being willing to leave behind the safe and secure place in the boat to step out into an uncertain future.

God may be calling you to do that right at this moment in time. Perhaps you are stuck at the point of saying 'What if...?' And if you are not careful you could still be there in ten, twenty or thirty years' time. Faith would not be faith if you had answers to all your questions before you made a move.

Throughout Scripture we find examples of people who were called to leave the safety of things they knew for the uncertainty of a future yet to be revealed.

* Abraham left his homeland for a new one (Genesis 12:1ff).

* Moses led a whole nation into a desert (Exodus 3:1ff).

* Joshua led them into the promised land when it was full of hostile people (Joshua 1:1ff).

* In the New Testament, Hebrews 11 is a chapter full of examples of people who left behind the safe, secure and predictable in order to receive God's best.

Moving out

Faith means stepping out on the basis of God's word. If you read Peter's story carefully you will notice that it was only when he heard Jesus' specific command, 'Come!' that Peter climbed over the side of the boat. There is a huge difference between faith and presumption, and the trouble is that often these days we confuse one with the other.

For example, I might believe that if I jumped from the roof of my house God would enable me to overcome, by faith, the law of gravity. I might be sincere in my belief. I may even show strong conviction about my faith, never wavering even for a moment. I could even demonstrate the courage that such an act would require. I might possess all these things and still be totally wrong!

That may sound far-fetched, so take an example from the news. There are numerous 'holy' wars to choose from, but take the long-running struggle involving Iran and Iraq. What makes teenage boys enlist to fight in such a war? What possesses these young Basij (volunteers) to be a human wave rushing in their hundreds against enemy lines, often totally unprotected? What makes a seventeen-year-old girl blow herself to pieces in a suicide mission by driving a car packed with explosives into an embassy wall? They believe that what they are doing is a glorious act of faith. They have been conditioned to the response that death in such a holy cause will mean instant access to paradise with all the eternal rewards due to a martyr.

But that is not faith—it is presumption. Examine the foundation of such a belief and you discover that it is as crazy as jumping off the roof.

It takes prayer, discernment and quite a bit of maturity to tell the difference between faith and presumption. That is why it is a wise safeguard to pray through your guidance with a leader you can trust.

When God speaks it is safe to step out. The other disciples watched in astonishment as Peter moved out in faith.

If you are going to serve God effectively then operate on this principle, 'Do whatever he tells you' (John 2:5).

Battling through

When you move out in faith, be prepared for an ongoing fight with fear. For Peter the hard part was not getting out of the boat, but staying afloat. We read that he walked on the water towards Jesus and, in the light of what happened, he must have got within an arm's length of him.

It was at this point that Peter noticed the violent storm and took his eyes off Jesus. He began to sink, but as he cried out the Lord reached over and caught his hand. 'You of little faith,' Jesus said, 'Why did you doubt?' (Matthew 14:31). Behind what appears to be a stinging reply, I believe there was a touch of humour in what

Jesus was saying. It took a great deal of faith to leap over the side of the boat and take those first hesitant steps on the waves. Peter had almost made it!

Fear and faith never reside comfortably side by side. That is where battling through becomes so important. In serving God there are times when the waves seem bigger than Jesus. Fear will tell you to panic and run; faith will tell you to stay put and trust. The writer to the Hebrews gives some good advice at this point, 'Let us fix our eyes on Jesus' (Hebrews 12:2). The way to battle through and win is to keep an unclouded picture of Jesus right in the centre of your vision.

Faith is indispensable if you are going to be effective in serving God. The early Christians didn't look for bank managers or accountants when they came to choosing leaders, but men full of faith and the Holy Spirit (see Acts 6:1ff). You may be a bank manager, but the essential ingredients go beyond professional expertise. One of the greatest needs in the church in Britain today is for men and women with faith and vision.

You have probably heard the one about the two shoe salesmen from rival companies who were sent to a remote island to establish their business among the natives. One cabled back to Head Office that he would be returning home because no one wore any shoes. The other cabled back for more samples, excited at the prospect of making a fortune! One saw problems, the other possibilities.

The Old Testament story of the spies in Canaan is all about faith (see Numbers 13:1ff). Two came back talking about grapes and ten came back talking about giants.

The two who saw God as being bigger than the problem actually made it into the promised land and, like Peter, they learned the lesson that when it comes to faith—you'd better not leave home without it.

Workout

1. 'Now faith is being sure of what we hope for and certain of what we do not see' (Hebrews 11:1). We have read some other definitions of faith too: 'Faith means believing God'; 'Faith often calls us to leave behind the security of things in which we trust'; 'Faith means stepping out on the basis of God's word'; 'Faith is indispensable if you are going to be effective in serving God.'

What does 'faith' mean to you? Give a definition from an example in your own life when you have exercised faith. What did God teach you through that experience?

2. Is your everyday life lived 'in faith'—believing God and trusting him? Or is faith just for special occasions? Be prepared to look for God working in your everyday situations. It will encourage your faith and enable you to trust him more.

Prayer

Father, I thank you for the excitement there is in trusting you. Thank you for being bigger than any problem. Help me to keep my eyes fixed on Jesus and to keep trusting and believing in your word. Thank you that you have shown me again and again that you are faithful and can be trusted. Amen.

PS

Against all hope, Abraham in hope believed...he did not waver through unbelief regarding the promise of God, but was strengthened in his faith and gave glory to God, being fully persuaded that God had power to do what he had promised (Romans 4:18, 20–21).

SECTION 4

Personal Evangelism

17

Right Place . . . Right Time

Reading

Acts 8:26–40

Think through

The plane was packed, but the seat next to mine was
empty. I stretched out and looked forward to the
prospect of sleeping a long flight away. Then she arrived.
'Is this seat 9F?' she enquired politely before depositing
herself and her baggage next to me.

I can't stand friendly types when I am trying to sleep,
but I figured a few polite pleasantries at that stage might
leave me free of chat for the rest of the journey. Then
she asked the fateful question: 'What do you do for a
living?' There was now no escape. 'Not *now*, Lord,' I
thought to myself, and then with the reluctance of a
furtive CIA agent I told her that I was an ambassador of
the good news (who secretly wanted a quiet sleep!).

And then it hit me. Evangelism—sharing Jesus—is
not just something you *do*, it is what you *are*. There is no
such thing as an off-duty disciple. God had brought me
to the right place at the right time.

My attitude changed and soon I was deep in conversation with a girl who had a lot of problems, a lot of questions and a bunch of Christian friends at university who had been praying for her for months. I felt bad. A reluctant servant who could have easily let a divine set-up dwindle with a few muttered comments about the weather.

I suspect a lot of us can identify with Becky Manley-Pippert, when she wrote in her book *Out of the Salt-Shaker* (IVP 1980): 'There was a part of me that secretly felt evangelism was something you shouldn't do to your dog, let alone a friend.'

We are going to take a look at a chapter in the book of Acts that teaches us a lesson we need to hear; evangelism isn't something you *do*, it's a *way of life*.

The person that God can use

Philip was an ordinary Christian. He had a special gift from God as an evangelist, but it is only later in his life that he is described in that way (Acts 21:8). His first appearance is where he is chosen as a 'deacon' to serve the church in Jerusalem in practical duties (Acts 6:5). He was a man 'full of the Spirit and wisdom' and, not surprisingly, it wasn't long before God used him in other ways. If you are faithful in the small routine things then God will extend your service for him.

He was led to take the good news of Jesus to Samaria (Acts 8:5) where miracles and changed lives were the demonstration of the Holy Spirit's power. We read that 'there was great joy in that city'. That is what makes it all the more surprising that God should move him from a place where it was all happening to a caravan route in the desert: 'Now an angel of the Lord said to Philip, "Go south to the road—the desert road—that goes down from Jerusalem to Gaza"' (Acts 8:26). It would be the equivalent of God telling you to leave your church where revival has just broken out after you have spoken at the Bible study, and stand on the hard shoulder of the M1 near Milton Keynes! But Philip understood the heart of God and the grip that Jesus had on his life was such that he was willing to obey what must have seemed a strange command.

It is a common temptation today to think of evangelism as something that you sit back and *watch*. It isn't. Shepherds don't produce sheep, they just look after them. In the reproductive process, sheep give birth to sheep. Forget the idea that evangelism is someone else's responsibility and face the question honestly: *are you available to God*?

The people who need to hear

So he started out, and on his way he met an Ethiopian eunuch, an important official in charge of all the treasury of Candace, queen of the Ethiopians. This man had gone to Jerusalem to worship, and on his way home was sitting in his chariot reading the book of Isaiah the prophet (Acts 8:27–28).

God had a man he wanted Philip to meet. He was an Ethiopian and was a high-ranking government minister. He was a God-fearer and was obviously searching for spiritual reality. He must have been desperate to have been struggling with a scroll from Isaiah in a language that wasn't his own, in the back of a bumpy chariot! He was a man with questions, and God planned to bring across his path a man who had some of the answers.

Some of us back off from sharing our faith in Jesus because we are afraid of being asked questions we can't answer. If that ever does happen there is nothing wrong in saying, 'I just don't know—but I'll find out.' But in fact the questions that we fear most are not always the ones that people are asking. God doesn't want you to be just a spiritual Bren gun, loaded up with all the right proof-texts just ready to spray the 'opposition' with well-rehearsed answers. He wants you to share *Jesus*—what you know of him, what he is doing in your life and how ordinary people can come to know an extraordinary God.

There are people everywhere who are searching. It could be that God wants to use you as a link in the chain of events leading someone else into the kingdom.

And be prepared for God to lead you to surprising people. Philip and the Ethiopian were vastly different in nationality, culture—and colour! Socially they would never have met up with each other, but God arranged the appointment. Pray for the sort of sensitivity that helps you to recognize people that God has allowed to cross your path.

The message we need to share

If you want to learn about how to give away your faith, then take a look at how Philip did it:

* *He began where he was at*

Philip started at the point where the Ethiopian was asking questions. And he opened up their conversation with a natural question: 'Then Philip ran up to the chariot and heard the man reading Isaiah the prophet. "Do you understand what you are reading?" Philip asked' (Acts 8:30). Systems, tracts and methods make great servants but hopeless masters. When Jesus met people he saw them as individuals, and as you will see from the gospels, his approach related directly to their need.

* *He shared about a person*

Philip doesn't seem to have mentioned the church in

Jerusalem with its 'thriving Sunday School' or the new church in Samaria with its 'ambitious new building project'... just Jesus.

The Ethiopian was already reading about him (Isaiah 53:7–8) when along came a man with the final piece of the jigsaw. Philip told him about Jesus, the suffering servant Isaiah described, who had given his life up as a ransom for imprisoned people but was now alive again.

As an Indian Christian once put it: 'We have been presenting Christianity the system not Christ the person... we have to present to the world the living Christ....'

* *He shared on the basis of God's truth*

The Bible is not a textbook *about* God, it is the living word *of* God. The 'sword of the Spirit' is given for battle, not to be hung over the mantelpiece. Sharing our personal experience is right, but remember there are thousands of people with 'personal experiences', for example, of the drug culture or the occult. What makes the Christian experience unique is that it is built on revealed truth from the Creator. Always anchor your story into His-story. And, by the way, if you do have a friend who is searching, the best book you can ever give them is a Bible.

* *He shared a message that called for action*

Although the complete details of their conversation are not recorded, it is obvious that Philip spelt out what commitment to Jesus Christ would mean. The Ethiopian wanted to be baptized as an open demonstration that he wanted to begin as a follower of Jesus. That took a lot of faith and courage as he was probably accompanied on his journey by other officials and possibly an armed guard. No one would have any doubts as to where he stood in relation to Jesus Christ (Acts 8:36).

Too often our personal witnessing can be little more than 'Smile—God loves you', without presenting the God who commands people to respond to his love with sacrificial obedience.

The miracles that we should expect

If early church tradition is reliable, the story of the Ethiopian does not end in Acts 8. He returned home and through his witness many others came to a living faith in Jesus Christ. The potential of one life dedicated to God is staggering. The Ethiopian was a key person and beyond him there lay a whole nation that needed to hear the gospel. The meeting that God arranged on that dusty desert road had far-reaching implications.

We need to pray for key people to come into the kingdom, and we need to pray with the sort of God-given faith that expects answers. But who are the key people? Not just public personalities, surely? God knows, and he will show you if you are open.

Perhaps that friend of yours with the hang-ups about a God of love and a world of suffering could, in God's purposes, become a pioneer missionary leader, another Billy Graham or....

Workout

1. Are you a secret Christian (at least, when surrounded by non-Christians)? We are *all* called to be witnesses to our faith. How many people do you come into contact with each day who don't know Jesus? Do you ask God for opportunities to share your faith with them?

2. Think through the good news that you have to share with people. Look at the characteristics of Philip's faith sharing: he began where the Ethiopian was at—not with a heavenly sales patter but by showing a genuine

interest in what the man was doing. He shared about a person—the central part of his faith was his relationship with Jesus. Is that true for you? He shared on the basis of God's truth—Philip didn't just share an experience, it was grounded in God's word. He shared a message that called for action—he stressed the need for a personal response. How do you share your faith?

3. A useful book for further reading is *Out of the Salt-Shaker* by Rebecca Manley-Pippert (IVP).

Prayer

Thank you, Father, for the freedom that we have to share our faith, and I ask your forgiveness that I waste that privilege so often. Father, thank you for the different people that you bring across my path—people that need to hear about you and see the reality of a life lived with Jesus at the centre. Please open up those opportunities for me to share my relationship with you by the power of your Holy Spirit living in me. Amen.

PS

Like Peter, who denied Christ by his silence while warming himself by the fire, we sometimes opt out of our responsibility.

John Stott wrote a book some years ago entitled *Our Guilty Silence* and in it comments:

> We should not lightly despise Peter, for we share his guilt too often. Indeed we are altogether too ready to find a scapegoat for our own guilty silence, and to blame everything and everybody except ourselves. (Hodder & Stoughton 1967, p. 118.)

18

Wage a Prayer War

Reading

1 Timothy 2:1–4

Think through

The baying mob is thirsty for blood. Armed with stones, sticks and home-made petrol bombs they have occupied the streets. Overturned cars have been set on fire. Soldiers and police shelter behind riot-shields as another fusillade of rocks hurtles through the night sky....

Confronted with that sort of crisis in Ulster's troubled streets, the British army had to come up with new methods of crowd control. One idea was to form themselves into 'snatch squads'. They would pinpoint the leaders of a riot and then in a concentrated charge into the crowd would grab the target and then withdraw with their captive. The philosophy was simple—snatch the leaders and you calm the crowd.

Christians could learn a great deal from that military tactic. We all agree that prayer is important, but so often fail to use the most powerful weapon that God has given us. Perhaps we feel defeated when we look at how poor our own level of praying has become. Maybe we are discouraged because our prayers sometimes seem to go unanswered. More often than not we have, at best, only a passing, nodding acquaintance with prayer. R. A. Torrey once wrote: 'There are few converted in this world, unless in connection with someone's prayers.' He goes on to relate his own testimony of how he was woken in the middle of the night and had a vivid encounter with God which led to his own conversion to Christ 'probably inside five minutes'. It was later that he discovered a friend at college who had committed himself to pray for Torrey until Jesus Christ became Lord of his life.

God invites—and commands—us to be involved with him in the work of changing people's lives. It is both a mystery and a miracle when a person becomes a Christian. The verses we are looking at in this chapter (1 Timothy 2:1–4) remind us of our need to get involved in praying for others.

God wants us to pray

'I urge, then, first of all, that requests, prayers, intercession and thanksgiving be made for everyone' (1 Timothy 2:1).

Paul is writing to Timothy, a young Christian leader. He is passing on instructions on how to lead the people of God. Paul is clear in spelling out the priorities. Christians are to get stuck in to the business of praying for others.

Paul uses different words to describe the activity of prayer, not because he wants to fill up the page or dazzle Timothy with his spiritual vocabulary, but to describe how broad and vast an experience prayer is meant to be. Look at the words he uses:

* Requests. The basic idea behind this word is a sense of need. Because we *need* something we *ask* God to supply it. People can't see their need of Jesus unless God opens their eyes, and we should pray for that to happen.

* Prayers. This is a comprehensive word which covers every form of approach we make to God. William Barclay writes: 'There are certain needs which only God can satisfy...it may well be that our weakness haunts us because we so often take our needs to the wrong place.'

* Intercession. This means pleading in the interests of others. It is a word used for offering a petition to a governor or king. We have the privilege and duty to bring others and their needs to God.

* Thanksgiving. Prayer doesn't just mean asking God for things but also thanking God for things. Our praying should always be wrapped in thanksgiving (see Philippians 4:6).

God wants us to pray for others

'...for everyone—for kings and all those in authority' (1 Timothy 2:1–2).

Time magazine announced its 'Man of the Year—1983' as a joint award shared between Presidents Reagan of the USA and Andropov of the USSR. The cover picture showed the two men facing in opposite directions. The point was clear. Here were the leaders of the two most powerful nations on the earth, armed to the teeth and refusing to talk to each other. Many people are afraid of that situation and the grim prospect for global survival.

But the *real* power and authority lies not in Moscow or Washington—but in heaven. 'All authority in heaven and on earth has been given to me,' declared Jesus (Matthew 28:18). It is in his name and in his authority we must pray. Our power to shape world events lies not in what we say when we are on our feet, but in what we pray when we are on our knees.

Chuck Colson, who worked in the White House in the Nixon era, has said: 'I discovered that authority is not in the palace of power but in the place of the powerless. God's power is superior to man's power.'

We need to pray for *leaders*. Try using the TV news as the agenda for your prayer meeting. Too many of us have a 'four walls' vision of the kingdom of God, and one way to remedy that is to turn our personal praying and prayer meetings into the powerhouses they can be.

We need to pray for *everyone*. All of us meet and work with non-Christians most days of the week. Make a list of the people who inhabit your 'world' and start to pray for them to come to know Jesus. Other people took time to pray for you and now you can be involved in building the kingdom by praying for others.

Author John White tells of the Emperor Napoleon and the way he would watch the development of his battles from a quiet vantage point, analysing the situation as he watched. His key general would watch with him. 'That farm,' he once said to Marshall Ney, 'that farm you can see on the ridge over there. Take it. Seize it. Hold it! For if you can the battle is won.'

If you aim at nothing—you'll hit it every time. Make your praying real, honest and specific.

God wants us to pray for others to be saved

'This is good, and pleases God our Saviour, who wants all men to be saved and to come to a knowledge of the truth' (1 Timothy 2:3–4).

God's heartbeat is for men and women. At the supermarket, in a tube train, on the terraces...those are the places that we can get near to the heart of God, because wherever people are, that is where God's heart is. God cares passionately about lost people, and he wants us to reflect his heart and care passionately about them as well.

That is why our prayers for others are to be specific rather than the 'bless 'em all' attitude that we sometimes adopt. We should pray for people to be saved and come to a knowledge of the truth. Don't be embarrassed about that little word 'saved'. It has been abused and misused by some, but it is a great biblical word describing the wholeness God wants people to discover in Jesus Christ. Forgiveness, power over sin, freedom from guilt, eternal life—all these themes and more besides—are contained in the word 'saved'.

Do you pray for people like that? Perhaps, like me, you want to get more involved in praying for others. Here are some practical suggestions:

1. Ask God who you need to be praying for

Don't make the list so long that you give up in despair! It is better to start with a few friends that you can pray for daily.

2. Pray for them regularly

Keep the list in a place where it will remind you to pray. (For example, stuck to the TV screen!)

3. Pray with others

One of the most exciting things to emerge out of Mission England was the Prayer Triplet scheme. Three Christians agree to meet at least once a week to pray together for three non-Christian friends each. God has done some remarkable things through this scheme. Praying with others can be a great encouragement.

4. *Pray in faith*

Open your heart up to the possibility of a miracle. Begin where you are, even if your faith only takes you as far as to ask that your friends begin to show an interest. Pray and believe God.

A word of warning: prayer is dynamite. People's lives could be changed, your own cosy routine disrupted and your spiritual life transformed. Be prepared for God to use *you* to answer your own prayers.

A friend of mine was visiting a church not long ago. He had woken in the middle of the previous night with a person's name ringing in his ears. He had no idea who the name belonged to but felt a strong urging from God to get out of bed and pray for that person immediately. My friend, being no spiritual giant who was used to getting words of knowledge in the middle of the night, confessed to feeling a little foolish as he knelt to pray for a person he wasn't even sure existed. The following day, at the close of the evening service, he was shaking hands with the congregation as they left church. A huge bear of a man shook my friend's hand so hard his tonsils almost rattled. 'W-w-what's your name?' my friend asked— feeling a nudge from God. The bear told him. My friend said, 'Well, I think you should know, God woke me in the middle of the night and told me to pray for you!'

The big man was pole-axed. He ran out into the night, and the preacher was convinced he'd made a big mistake. But he came back. A man who had been running from God for years came into the family. The bear became a lamb.

That's the thing about prayer—it's the most powerful weapon we have.

Workout

1. After the practical suggestions comes the practical application! It's so easy to accept something as a good idea in theory, but then get side-tracked and never put that good idea into action. Take time *now* to ask God who you need to be praying for. Write their names down and make a commitment to pray for those people.

2. Is it possible for you to meet with one or two friends to pray together—maybe over coffee, or in your lunch hour . . . or even before work in the early morning? Don't be afraid to make the first move and ask someone to pray with you.

Prayer

Dear Father, thank you that you love to hear my prayers. Help me to be aware of the preparation that you have already started in the lives of my friends and keep me open to your promptings to pray for them. Thank you for the privilege of working *with* you in bringing people to be saved by you. Amen.

PS

No prayer is made by man alone:
   The Holy Spirit pleads;
And Jesus, on the eternal throne,
   For sinners intercedes.

O thou by whom we come to God,
   The Life, the Truth, the Way,
The path of prayer thyself hast trod:
   Lord, teach us how to pray!

James Montgomery

19

What Is the Gospel?

Reading

1 Corinthians 15:1–28

Think through

He looked like a walking Bible bookshop. His jacket
was emblazoned with stickers, tracts were bulging from
his pockets and he had a large, regulation black leather
Bible under his arm. He carried a banner bearing the
simple message: '*Smile—Jesus loves you!*' A group of
punks had stopped to listen. One of them seemed
transfixed by what the earnest young man was saying.
The punk ambled across, tapped the banner and broke
into a toothy, fixed grin. 'OK, mate,' he said, holding the
smile as if he had a coat-hanger wedged in his mouth, 'so
I'm smiling. Now what do I do?'

You may have grasped the fact that you are an ambassador of Christ, but are you absolutely clear about the
message you have been given to pass on? The verses we
are looking at in this chapter take us back to basics, and
it is worth checking out that we are sharing *the* good
news, and not our own watered-down version of it.

The Corinthian Christians had problems about the resurrection of the body. In this difficult but meaty chapter, Paul is proving the nonsense of such a claim. He argues that the resurrection of Jesus is a gospel 'basic' and if Christ has been raised back to life then it follows that we shall experience resurrection as well (1 Corinthians 15:12–19).

He reminds the Corinthians about the gospel taught to them when they first believed (1 Corinthians 15:1–8). Look at some of the basics that Paul spells out:

1. The gospel is not man-made but God-given

'For what I received I passed on to you as of first importance...' (1 Corinthians 15:3).

Paul did not invent the gospel, nor was it taught to him by the other apostles. He received it by a revelation from Jesus Christ (see Galatians 1:11–24). Simply believing God-facts does not make someone a Christian. The Holy Spirit reveals our need of Jesus Christ and causes us to reach out to him in faith.

2. The gospel is about a person—Jesus Christ

Paul deliberately uses the word 'Christ' in 1 Corinthians 15:3. The Greek word is *Christos* which means 'Messiah' or 'Anointed One'. Jesus was more than a man—he was the Son of God, the long-promised Messiah, the Anointed One. Satan is skilful in diverting us up cul-de-sacs of theological speculation and it is easy for us to get side-tracked. Make sure when you share the gospel that you concentrate on the person that matters: Jesus Christ (see Acts 8:35).

3. The gospel focuses on the death and resurrection of Jesus Christ

Paul recaps on the good news the Corinthians had received and believed:

* *The fact of his death*. 'Christ died...' (1 Corinthians 15:3). Good Friday was horribly real. The lashes were real, the nails were real, the suffering, blood and spiritual agony were all real.

When one of my sons was about three years old, some friends came to visit us on Good Friday. Earlier in the day I had been trying to answer some of his simple and sincere questions about why it was a special day. The door opened, and our friends walked in. He rushed over to meet them and shouted out—'D'you know what? God died today!'

* *The reason for his death*. 'Christ died for our sins...' (1 Corinthians 15:3). The fact of his death is profound, but the reason is so simple. He died for our sins. People need that clearly, lovingly and personally explained to them (see Romans 5:6–8).

* *The reality of his death*. '...that he was buried...' (1 Corinthians 15:4). The death of Jesus Christ was not a faked event. He did not faint on the cross and then later revive in the cold of the tomb. Witnesses saw him die. They saw the body taken down from the cross, wrapped in grave-clothes and placed in a tomb with a sealed entrance with armed guards around it.

* *The truth of his resurrection*. '...that he was raised on the third day... and that he appeared...' (1 Corinthians 15:4–7).

It's quite a list of witnesses: Peter, 500 brothers at the same time, James and Paul—and that's not all of them! Christ rose from the dead and is alive today. The evidence is not just an empty tomb but a resurrected body which the disciples saw with their own eyes.

4. The gospel is the fulfilment of God's promise

'...according to the Scriptures...' (1 Corinthians 15:4).

God's rescue plan for people did not 'just happen', it was prophesied hundreds of years before. Many Old Testament passages point to the birth, life, death and resurrection of the Messiah. Study Psalm 22 as just one example. Quoted by Jesus from the cross, this Psalm describes the agony and sense of desolation he was passing through. It accurately describes the physical details of crucifixion. (All the more remarkable when you consider that crucifixion had not been invented at this time!) The death and resurrection of Jesus were no accident—but rather the climax of God's great rescue plan.

Workout

How do you shape up in sharing the good news? If you want to learn how to communicate more effectively here are some helpful guidelines:

1. Get to know your Bible

Know why and what you believe by getting to grips with God's truth. How would you explain the gospel to someone with no church connections, that is, in everyday language?

2. Stop hiding behind (borrowed) jargon

It is easy to slip into clichés. Examine what you say when you are sharing your own testimony, and ask yourself the question: 'If I wasn't a Christian could *I* understand it?'

3. Read good evangelistic books

There are some excellent books written for non-Christians, and it would do *you* good to read them. Just by seeing how gifted communicators get the message across will help you to grasp the gospel and get an idea of how to share it in everyday language. Some examples are:

Right with God by John Blanchard (Banner of Truth).
Basic Christianity by John Stott (IVP).
I Want to be a Christian by J. I. Packer (Kingsway).
Finding Faith by Andrew Knowles (Lion).
Evidence that Demands a Verdict by Josh McDowell
    (Scripture Press).

Prayer

Thank you, dear Lord, for the good news that we have to share. Thank you for that message which can be grasped by a child and yet leave the world's most brilliant minds in turmoil trying to comprehend the mystery that 'God died'. Give me a greater understanding and the ability to share the gospel with people around me. Amen.

PS

For what I received I passed on to you as of first importance: that Christ died for our sins according to the Scriptures, that he was buried, that he was raised on the third day according to the Scriptures (1 Corinthians 15:3–4).

20

New Christians Need Care

Reading

Acts 18:24–28

Think through

He was young, a bit cocky and very confused. He'd seen quite a large slice of life and that had left him with a lot of questions. At his university there was a student who was just a couple of years older. A friend put them in touch and suggested they met up. There was nothing formal about their get-togethers—just a couple of young people facing their faith with honest questions and looking at the Bible for the answers. They met for a whole year— once a week—sometimes for up to three hours at a time.

Looking back, years later, the younger Christian commented: 'It is impossible to stress how vital these sessions were for me. Without them, humanly speaking, I should never have survived as a Christian.'

I, for one, am very glad that someone took time out to care for the young David Watson. The older friend was David Sheppard (now Bishop of Liverpool) and his nurture of one young student laid a firm foundation for a fruitful ministry.

New Christians need care. That slogan needs to be written in letters ten feet high and hung at the front of every church.

That care is best demonstrated on a one-to-one basis, and this changes the picture quite a good deal. We all agree that follow-up is essential for new Christians, but somehow we feel it is someone else's responsibility. Wrong. The responsibility belongs to you and me.

Take the story of Apollos, Priscilla and Aquila as a practical case study (see Acts 18:24–28). Now Apollos was not your average new Christian. He was a learned man (verse 24), he had a thorough knowledge of the Scriptures (verse 24), and he had been instructed in the way of the Lord (verse 25).

But, in spite of all this, we read 'he knew only the baptism of John', which probably means that he had only grasped part of the gospel message. When the husband and wife team of Priscilla and Aquila heard him, they did not throw up their hands in horror that someone who was so new in the faith was teaching and preaching. They didn't even indulge in the Christian pastime of criticism. We read that they did two things to help Apollos grow up in his faith:

1. They opened their home

People in the early church used their homes freely. Jesus broke bread with his disciples in an upper room—obviously part of a home. The Jerusalem church followed the pattern by breaking bread in their homes as well (Acts 2:46).

Church buildings—if used properly—can be a blessing, but so often they can become a barrier. New believers need teaching and training, and for that to happen we need to share more with them than an hour's shoulder-rubbing in the pew each Sunday.

2. *They opened their hearts*

Priscilla and Aquila took time with Apollos and 'explained to him the way of God more adequately' (verse 26). There were gaps in his understanding that needed to be filled in, and that needed sensitive handling. Sometimes in seeking to put people right we can so easily end up putting them down. God used their bridge of friendship to clear up the problem for Apollos and soon he was greatly used in teaching and explaining the gospel to others (verse 28).

In the animal kingdom it is sheep that produce sheep —not the shepherds! God may have given good leadership in your church, but the task of discipling new believers belongs to you as much as to your minister or youth leader.

Perhaps you have a friend who has recently become a Christian. Instead of simply taking him to church, and expecting growth to just happen, how about spending quality time alongside him, helping his relationship with Jesus to grow? In other words, get into the spiritual reproduction business. It is a challenge, because you have to be walking close to the Lord yourself in order to be effective in helping others.

Perhaps you can look back in your own life and remember people who spent time with you when you first became a Christian. Now you have a chance to pay back that kindness by being available to help a newcomer to the family.

And in case you feel tempted to hide behind the excuse: 'I don't know enough about my faith yet,' remember that you actually only have to be one step ahead of another person in order to help them.

Have you got a friend who is a new Christian? Here are some ways to get started on a friendship that can make a disciple:

Fix a regular time to meet

It is easy to let things drift after an enthusiastic start. Make a regular commitment—and stick to it.

Assume nothing

One of the best ways to de-jargonize your vocabulary is to spend time with a new Christian. Begin with basics. Ask your Christian bookshop for details of Bible study books for new Christians (probably the Navigator Press is one of the best in this field).

Focus on the Bible

Relate all you talk about to Scripture, otherwise you run the risk of becoming very experience-centred.

Bring truth to life

Help your friend to see how God's truth relates to everyday living and explain how this works out in your own life.

Be open

How helpful it is to be honest about temptation, failure and sin. How even more helpful to know that God has led you through some of those barriers. Learn to be honest as you share.

Be prepared for set-back

Problems, doubts, fears and difficulties are all part of the normal Christian walk. The secret is learning to stick by people and see them through to the other side.

Push them out of the nest

Don't let anyone become so dependent on you that you become a substitute saviour. It can and does happen. As you see your friend growing in his faith, encourage him to relate to other Christians and get involved in serving God in practical ways.

C. S. Lewis once defined his role as a Christian writer as an adjective, humbly striving to point others to the noun of truth. That is a lovely way of expressing how God has provided for us to grow in our knowledge of himself.

And to be frank—the Christian church in Britain is in desperate need of adjectives. Any offers?

Workout

1. Would you be willing to care for a new Christian? New babies need a lot of attention and care if they are going to grow. Would you be willing to give the necessary time?

2. Now think about things practically. Is there a new Christian that you know who needs that encouragement? If not, how about asking your minister or church leaders if you can be of any help in a discipleship group or meeting with someone on a one-to-one basis? (Failing that, how about praying for people to become Christians?!)

3. There's no harm in starting to prepare yourself now. Look through some of the Bible study books for new Christians, try thinking through some of the questions that new Christians raise, and think through the things that helped you most when you first became a Christian.

Prayer

Please forgive me, Father, for often neglecting the responsibility that you have given each one of your children—to care for each other. Father, please draw me closer to yourself and give me the ability to share what you have taught me—show me the person you want me to get alongside and help me to care for this person and help them to grow as a Christian. Thank you, Father. Amen.

PS

> For we are all a part of one another,
> We cannot hope to live life fully on our own;
> We each possess a precious part of our Father's nature,
> And together we'll become that perfect whole.
>
> So let us open up ourselves to one another
> Without fear of being hurt or turned away;
> For we need to confess our weaknesses,
> To be covered by our brother's love,
> To be real and learn our true identity.

Pat Bilbrough, *Let us open up ourselves*, copyright © Thankyou Music 1980. Used by permission.

SECTION 5

Sharp Edges—
Things that Make Us Hurt

21

Coping With Regret

Readings

1 Samuel 15:1–35; 16:1–5

Think through

We were going round in circles. No matter what was said he kept going on about what had gone wrong and who was responsible. He was beginning to sound like a record with the needle stuck. One thing was certain—until he buried the past, there was not much hope for the future.

Have you ever been in that situation? Unable to go forward as a Christian perhaps because of something that happened or something that was said to you? Too many Christians are paralysed by the past. Maybe you look back on lost opportunities, a situation that you feel you messed up badly—or just the fact that you wish you'd become a Christian a long time before you did.

Regret can be a crippling disease. Don't get me wrong, there must always be a large element of regret in true repentance, and it is right that we look back in sober reflection when we have stepped out of God's will.

What I'm speaking about is the tendency that some of us have to get locked into a very self-centred attitude to the past. I call it the 'if only' syndrome. 'If only that relationship had worked out...', 'If only I hadn't said that...', 'If only I could go back and start over again...'. It's a terrible trap to fall into.

A few weeks ago a friend of mine who is a paraplegic came to dinner. We have been friends for years and in many senses I tend to forget that he is in a wheelchair. But for my children it was a fascinating experience to have someone skidding around the house who could do wheelies! Inevitably the questions started tumbling out about why his legs don't work. I soon found myself explaining about the serious road accident that happened when he was a little boy, and the fact that from the waist down he was paralysed.

In some ways that is a picture of what a wrong sense of regret can do. It's like being hit by a truck and left with a very important part of you paralysed. You can be prevented from moving on in all that God has for you by looking back and thinking about what might have been.

Christian leaders are not immune to the 'if only' syndrome. Take Samuel—God's spokesman to Israel—as one example. Saul had been appointed as King but through disobedience had disqualified himself as a leader of God's people.

Samuel brought that message from God to the King: 'The Lord has torn the kingdom of Israel from you today and has given it to one of your neighbours—to one better than you' (1 Samuel 15:28). Then in the last verse of the same chapter we read these tragic words: 'Until the day Samuel died, he did not go to see Saul again, though Samuel mourned for him' (verse 35).

The word 'mourned' paints a powerful picture. Samuel was broken up by the tragedy, as if he had lost someone very close to him. So great was that heartbreak, he could not even face Saul again.

We can guess a little of what was going on in Samuel's mind. Did he feel a sense of personal failure as the man who had appointed him as King? Was there a shadow of guilt that he hadn't given Saul all the spiritual counsel he needed? Certainly the whole sorry mess of a king who had gone wrong and the potential damage that this could do to the nation was playing on his mind. Without much doubt, Samuel found himself thinking 'if only...'.

But notice how God deals with sorry servants. In the first verse of the next chapter (1 Samuel 16:1) God asks Samuel a hard question: 'How long will you mourn for Saul?' Then comes a fresh set of instructions: 'Fill your horn with oil and be on your way.' God had found a new king and Samuel was being sent to announce the choice.

We have all heard the saying: 'It's no use crying over spilt milk,' and in many ways that was God's antidote to Samuel's regret. The past is the past—get up and get going. Samuel was paralysed—unable to move ahead in God's purposes—because he was looking over his shoulder.

Now I am *not* saying we should minimize things that have gone tragically wrong. Nor am I trying to soft-pedal the God-given sense of repentance that comes to us when we have wandered off his pathway. But there are many Christians who are unable to go forward in their experience of God because they are bound up in the past.

I recently received a letter from a friend who is in that exact situation. I share with you what I replied to her: '"Today" is one of the great words in the Christian's vocabulary. Thank God for yesterday, trust God for tomorrow—but, by faith, get on with living for Jesus *today*.'

Whatever it is that has trapped you into the 'if only' syndrome, give it to God. Confess, and put right the things that are in your power to sort out. But refuse to get left behind. If God has truly buried the past, stop trying to dig it up again!

Workout

1. There is a famous song which says, 'I have no regrets,' but very few of us would say that's true. Are there moments, conversations or events in your life that you wish had never happened? Maybe those things have come to your mind as you've read through this chapter?

2. Do you find yourself stuck in the 'if only' syndrome? The good news is that however long ago this event was, or however bad it was, God does have the answer. That may sound trite, but it's true!

Here's a step-by-step guide to dealing with the 'if only' syndrome:

Take it to God

If God shows you some area of sin, confess it and put it right with him. 'If we confess our sins, he is faithful and just and will forgive us our sins and purify us from all unrighteousness' (1 John 1:9).

Put it right with your brother

If you know that there is a barrier between you and another Christian, contact him and sort it out as far as it is within your power.

> Therefore, if you are offering your gift at the altar and there remember that your brother has something against you, leave the gift there in front of the altar. First go and be reconciled to your brother; then come and offer your gift (Matthew 5:23–24).

Talk it over with yourself

If there are lessons you can learn, make sure you know what they are.

Talk it over with someone else

Sometimes the disappointment and frustration we feel needs to be unloaded—find a sympathetic friend with an open ear.

Put it behind you

Learn from the situation and, by faith, move on from it. God has new territory for you to cover. 'Forgetting what is behind and straining towards what is ahead, I press on' (Philippians 3:13).

Prayer

Thank you, Father, for the experiences you have taken me through; for all those things that you have woven together that make my life unique. Help me to learn from every aspect of the life you have given me and to be stronger in my relationship with you as a result. Amen.

PS

> Lay down your failures and excuses,
> All of the dreams that never come true.
> The past is a crutch you've been using,
> It's time you broke that thing in two.
> Open your eyes to tomorrow.
> Open your life to his care.
> Open your past to his mercy.
> Open your heart, he'll be there.
>
> Yesterday's gone now forever,
> We'll never change a thing we've done.
> But the guilt is behind us,

If our heart's moving on.
Never give an inch, just believe me,
What God's said, he's gonna do,
And he said when he started
He's never gonna quit 'til he's through.

Amy Grant, Gary Chapman, Bruce Hibbard, *Tomorrow*, copyright © Kenwood/Meadowgreen Music 1984. Used by permission.

22

When Doubt Strikes

Reading

Luke 7:18–23

Think through

A prison cell can be the loneliest place on earth. With so much time on your hands, problems can grow ten times larger than they really are, and the growing fear of an uncertain future means that the nightmares continue, even when you are wide awake. Day after day the long hours creep lazily by. Life goes on busily outside, but in prison it's like a bad film in slow motion.

John the Baptist found King Herod's prison at the Fort of Machaerus a wasting experience. The prophet of fire, action and wide open spaces found his congregation gone and his home an uncomfortable prison cell. Herod had thrown John into jail because he insisted on mixing politics with religion. It's no problem if you simply tell people to believe in God and be kind to each other—but when you start denouncing a king's morals and point to his private life as an example of sin...that's when the preaching has to stop (Luke 3:19–20)!

The months passed by and the doubts began to gnaw away at John's heart: 'Why doesn't God do something to help me—is he deaf?'; 'Perhaps Jesus of Nazareth is not the true Messiah'; 'It's not turning out as I expected—did I get my guidance wrong?'; 'Is the whole business of trusting God a delusion?'

News was reaching John of the mighty miracles Jesus was performing. The latest story was almost beyond belief: a dead man had been raised to life in a town called Nain, and the country was ablaze with rumours about the young carpenter from Nazareth who many claimed was the Messiah.

But I believe John had his doubts. He remembered the prophetic word God had entrusted to him. He was to be the forerunner of Christ—his job was to prepare the way of the Lord and then to get out of the way of the Lord. His message was for people to prepare for the Messiah. He would baptize with the Holy Spirit and fire. He would cut down unfruitful trees and sort the wheat from the chaff. His judgement would be of unquenchable fire. John's message was so strong, it even made him tremble. He had publicly identified Jesus of Nazareth as the one who was 'the Lamb of God, who takes away the sin of the world' (John 1:29).

Jesus, however, didn't quite fit his ideas, and, fearing the worst, John had sent his two disciples to ask Jesus the soul-searching question, 'Are you the one who was to come, or should we expect someone else?' (Luke 7:19).

Doubts hit us all at one time or another—and they are nothing to be ashamed of. Whether they are prompted by an unbelieving bishop on the TV or a cynical science teacher at school, doubts are going to hit you at various stages of your Christian life. Learn to expect them and you will be better equipped to handle them.

When doubt strikes

For John, prison was a special time of testing—just as we all face certain times of testing, although maybe not in prison. Here are some of the occasions when we are especially vulnerable to doubt:

When we are wrestling with intellectual problems

The Christian faith *is* reasonable, but we will face a barrage of critics who will claim it is anything but that! That is why we need a good grasp of the Bible, the background to it and a clear understanding of what we believe and why we believe it.

When God doesn't act in the way we expect

This was the heart of John the Baptist's problem. God seemed to be on strike, and his seeming inaction left John questioning his guidance.

When bad things happen to good people

Tragedy always throws us back to what we believe. And when inexplicable, unfair things happen in our world, we naturally ask questions about God and his power to control events.

When we are under spiritual attack

Doubt is a weapon that Satan uses frequently. Doubt is normal in the Christian life, but unbelief is sin, and Satan often skilfully employs doubt as a lever to lift us into unbelief. We must learn to resist him (see 1 Peter 5:8–9).

How you can cope

Look at the way Jesus dealt with John the Baptist. There was no heavy-handed condemnation, but loving encouragement (Luke 7:22). He tells John's disciples to report what they have 'seen and heard' and with that he sends a kind of coded message to his friend.

This message about the blind seeing, the lame walking, the lepers being cleansed, the deaf hearing and the dead being raised had special meaning. And the phrase 'and the good news is preached to the poor' added to that meaning. John—as a prophet—was steeped in the Old Testament Scriptures. These words, used deliberately, echoed prophecies such as Isaiah 35:5–6 and Isaiah 61:1. The coded message for John would be plain: 'Do you remember these prophecies concerning me? They are being fulfilled today. I am the Messiah.'

Jesus leads his friend back to the word of God which represents the very character of God. But he also sends the two disciples back with a personal message of encouragement: 'Blessed is the one who does not lose his faith in me' (Luke 7:23, Living Bible). Jesus reminds John that God has a special blessing for those who battle through doubt with faith, and trust God for the things they find hard to explain.

As a new Christian I remember groaning at the cliché: 'Feed your faith and starve your doubts to death.' A little older and (I hope) wiser I have found it to be absolutely true.

Faith needs feeding through the word of God, worship, prayer, commitment to a local church, the discipline of study and the exercise of service.

Faith needs nurturing through honest fellowship with friends who can encourage, through suffering, disappointments and times of spiritual dryness. And God—who alone knows best—tells us that *faith needs testing*. John, in his lonely prison cell, found that to be the case. And he discovered God's strength in his darkest moments of doubt.

Workout

1. Are there doubts that you are facing now? Can you pinpoint the reason behind those doubts? Don't be afraid to tell God about them. It's often in the act of expressing our doubts to him that we come to see them with God's perspective.

2. Don't allow yourself the luxury of wallowing in your doubts! It's so easy to get caught in a downward spiral of feelings when you start to dwell on negative thoughts. It makes sense to do something positive first. Look at some of the positive things that have been mentioned earlier in the chapter that you can do to feed your faith (and starve your doubts).

3. Remember, 'Doubt is normal in the Christian life, but unbelief is sin.' Satan would make us believe that we're the only person to have such doubts. Find a Christian friend/leader with whom you can talk things through. (If you are studying this within a group it may help you to express any doubts you have to each other, discuss them and pray about them together.)

Prayer

Dear Father, please forgive me for doubting you when you've constantly shown your love and faithfulness to me. Please help me to face my doubts and express them, instead of allowing them to fester and grow. Thank you that you see all things—past, present and future. My finite mind might not always understand completely what you're doing, but help me to learn to trust you in those questioning times. Amen.

PS

When you're up against a struggle
That shatters all your dreams
And your hopes have been cruelly crushed by Satan's
     manifested schemes
And you feel the urge within you to submit to
     earthly fear
Don't let the faith you're standing on seem to disappear.

Praise the Lord, God can work through those who praise Him.
Praise the Lord—for our God inhabits praise.
Praise the Lord—for the chains that seem to bind you
Serve only to remind you that they fall
Powerless behind you when you praise Him.

Praise the Lord by Brown Bannister & Mike Hudson. © Bug & Bear Music/Home Sweet Home Music/Kenwood Music. Used by permission.

23

Failure

Readings

Acts 13:1–13; 15:36–41

Think through

It may be losing your job, messing up your driving test or
being ditched by your girlfriend—whatever the circumstances, failure leaves a nasty taste in the mouth. Perhaps
you have known what it is to wait for weeks until, at last,
the postman delivers the small brown envelope with
familiar writing on the front. Eagerly you rip it open,
only to have your worst, nagging fears confirmed. There,
for all the world to read, in block capitals on a computer
print-out: FAILED.

At some point in your life you are going to meet with
failure. That is not a negative, faith-demeaning
statement, just an honest reflection on the experiences
of Christian people, both in the Bible and out of it.
Failure doesn't necessarily mean that you have sinned or
that God has stopped loving you. Once you have learned
to accept that failure is part of being human you are in a
strong position to face it as a Christian.

John Mark—the first Christian failure?

John Mark is an interesting, semi-anonymous character in the New Testament. He knew about failure first-hand, but instead of allowing it to crush him he saw God use it as a wonderful means of developing his character as a Christian and his ministry as a servant.

He was given the unique privilege of joining Barnabas and Saul (soon to become known almost exclusively as Paul) on the first organized missionary venture of the early church (see Acts 13:5). He was not in the big league of apostolic preachers, but went along as a sort of first-century 'roadie'.

Their first stop was in Cyprus where immediately they met satanic opposition to their message. Paul—who was never one to mince his words—confronted the occultic prophet who sought to stand against them and denounced him as a 'child of the devil' who was trying to get in the way of God's work. To add to that, the man, Elymas, was struck blind for such opposition. What a way for the church's first missionary trip overseas to begin!

Immediately after this incident, Luke records (without any explanation) that having sailed from Cyprus 'John left them to return to Jerusalem' (Acts 13:13).

A lot of eminently qualified people have speculated as to what made John Mark pull out of the trip, almost before it had begun. Was it homesickness, recurring bad health or just a realization that he hated travelling and constantly being on the move? Did John find Paul's approach to Elymas, the sorcerer, too much to handle? Or was he overwhelmed with feelings of inadequacy and an inability to cope alongside two spiritual giants?

We can't be sure of an accurate answer this side of heaven, but one thing we can all identify with is the dreadful feeling of failure that must have hung over him like a black cloud. John Mark had to go back to the church at Antioch where, just a few weeks before with a good deal of fuss and interest, he had been sent out on his task. Imagine trying to explain that to the deacons!

To compound John Mark's sense of failure, Paul and Barnabas fell out with each other over the issue of whether or not he should be allowed a 'second chance' to go with them. It was such a sharp disagreement that Paul and his ministry companion parted company and, so far as we can tell, they never worked together again (see Acts 15:36–41). Paul chose a new partner—Silas—and embarked on his second missionary journey. Meanwhile, Barnabas—perhaps with a flash of spiritual insight—took John Mark with him to Cyprus. Back to the very place where he had started out in his service for God. There was a lot to be sorted out in his life, but God is an expert in that department!

Scripture is silent on the subject of how God led John Mark to a point where he could come to terms with his failure and then move on. But two things that we do know are extremely important:

1. His relationship with Paul was restored

Some years after the split, Paul tells the Colossian church to welcome Mark (Colossians 4:10). But, most significantly, at the end of Paul's life he writes these words to Timothy: 'Get Mark and bring him with you, because he is helpful to me in my ministry' (2 Timothy 4:11). A few years earlier, Paul had refused to take John Mark with him on the grounds that he was a hindrance, and now he is asking that he joins him in his imprisonment because he is such a help! What made the difference? Grace. Both John Mark and Paul had learned about trusting in the grace of God to cover past weaknesses and failure.

2. He moved on from failure to growth

If we are honest, we know when we have sinned and broken fellowship with God. But have you realized that just as we have sinned in falling over, we sin when we insist on staying down? There is nothing super-spiritual about feeling a failure for the rest of your days, believing you can slink into heaven by the back door with no one noticing you. Scripture tells us: 'Where sin increased, grace increased all the more' (Romans 5:20). Agree with God about your failure. If he shows it up to be sin, confess it and seek to put matters right. But refuse with all your might to stay lying down.

Mark's gospel in the New Testament was written by John Mark, and he wrote it under the strong influence of Peter. Mark the failure became a valued co-worker with Paul and Peter, the two leading figures in the growth and development of the early Christian church. He refused to stay lying down.

John Newton was a slave trader who had a dramatic encounter with Jesus Christ, and went on to be an influential leader in the British church in the eighteenth century. He once talked about three 'wonders' he would experience in heaven.

> First, I will wonder at those who are there that I didn't think would be there. Then I will wonder at those who I thought would be there that are not there. But the third and greatest wonder of all will be that I am there at all!

That sounds like a man who knows quite a bit about failure—and a whole lot more about the grace of God.

Strange as it may seem, those things that you think disqualify you from receiving God's grace actually qualify you for it. Ask God to show you that, and next time you fail, get up—and *go on!*

Workout

1. Failure can hit us at a number of levels: we can fail ourselves; we can fail others; we can fail God. Take time to list examples of failure in your life. Some of these things may have happened a long while ago but still gnaw away at you and drag you down. Bring each one of these failures to God, confess them as sin (if they are) and then know God's forgiveness and restoration. (It may mean some practical forgiveness and restoration on your part too—either in the way you see yourself or because it makes you see how you have treated others who have failed in your eyes.)

2. God can teach us so much through our failure. As we bring the events of the past to him he can help us face the future positively, in his strength and in the strength of all that we have learned today.

Prayer

Father, you know there has been quite a lot of failure in my life—certain things that have happened that I'm still ashamed and embarrassed to talk about now. Thank you that your grace, your undeserved mercy and goodness, will enable me to put my failures behind me and go on with you. Thank you too for what it teaches me about the importance of staying close to you. Amen.

PS

The words of one of John Newton's most famous hymns sum this chapter up:

> Amazing grace! How sweet the sound
> That saved a wretch like me!

I once was lost, but now am found;
Was blind, but now I see.

'Twas grace that taught my heart to fear,
And grace my fears relieved;
How precious did that grace appear
The hour I first believed!

Through many dangers, toils and snares
I have already come;
'Tis grace has brought me safe thus far,
And grace will lead me home.

24

Facing Fear

Readings

Genesis 12:10–20; 1 John 4:18

Think through

They were about twenty minutes into the flight on a
routine short hop to London Heathrow. It was a filthy
night. Snow was forecast for most of the route, but apart
from the weather it was an ordinary flight in every way.
The message that came over the radio was a little
unusual, but gave no clue to the sense of panic some on
the ground were feeling.

'Flight RT 791—How many passengers do you have
on board?' the radio crackled. 'Thirty-seven plus crew,'
the captain replied. 'What is the nature of your enquiry?'
he pressed. There was a long silence during which
suggestions were being passed back and forth among
those on the ground taking charge in the emergency. At
last the radio burst into life once more with the disturbing
message, 'You are the subject of an IRA bomb threat—
it's a Class 1.'

My friend was the captain that night. He tells me that in fifteen seconds his life floated before him. He didn't want to die, and the carnage of a mid-air explosion made him shudder with fear. But then, a sense of peace and the presence of God flooded over him. As he put it afterwards, 'I just felt absolutely secure in my relationship with God.' That is what I call confidence. It comes from a sense of love, and love is God's perfect answer to fear.

Facing fear

We all battle with fears. Some are more panic-prone than others, no doubt, but to experience fear is part of fallen human nature. We were not created to live with fears, but sin and rebellion produce lives alienated from God. And life lived away from God is a breeding ground for fear. Fear of death, especially the process of dying, is common. Perhaps you fear exams, walking into a crowded room or being in a confined space. Anxiety about spiders, heights and animals can be seen as 'normal'—unless the fear is so excessive that it interferes with everyday living.

There are people who are bound up by Satan in all sorts of fears from which the Lord Jesus Christ can deliver them and bring the freedom of God's love.

> The Spirit of the Lord is on me, because he has anointed me to preach good news to the poor. He has sent me to proclaim freedom for the prisoners and recovery of sight for the blind, to release the oppressed, to proclaim the year of the Lord's favour (Luke 4:18–19).

But what about the everyday fears that we all battle with? Are we programmed to spend the rest of our lives with them? Not if the Bible is to be believed: 'There is no fear in love. But perfect love drives out fear…the man who fears is not made perfect in love' (1 John 4:18).

I remember once being in a prayer meeting when someone shared a paranoid fear of going to the dentist. He went on to explain how God had brought him to a situation where he could face up to the fear and overcome it. I kept quiet, but found what was shared so appropriate to my own fears. It was a liberating experience. I discovered that God actually could set us free from fear—even those embarrassing anxieties that we feel certain are unique to us.

One of the things that gives the Bible a ring of truth is the way in which it gives us pictures of *real* people. Moses was so meek, and yet he lost his temper. David was a spiritual giant, but he walked into terrible moral failure. Elijah stood strong against satanic forces, and then ran from the mumbled threats of a woman. Peter, James and John were fishermen, and the picture the gospels paint of them is so real you can almost smell the sweat!

Abraham is seen as the man of faith. He is known as 'the father of all who believe'. How encouraging to know that the man of faith had to battle with fear.

In Genesis 12:10–20 we read that Abram (as he was still called at the time) was living in Egypt because of a famine in Canaan. He tried to pass off his wife, Sarah, as his sister. She was a beautiful woman and Abram, in his irrational fear, felt certain that the Egyptians would kill him out of lust for her. He persuaded her to join his conspiracy of cowardice, 'so that I will be treated well for your sake and my life will be spared because of you' (verse 13). You can read for yourself how Pharaoh took her into his palace, and the terrible consequences that followed. A red-faced Abram left Egypt with his credibility in tatters and, no doubt, his relationship with Sarah damaged.

This particular fear gripped Abram again (see Genesis 20:1–18) and interestingly enough his son Isaac faced the same battle (see Genesis 26:1–11). Abraham, the man who believed God's promise, which ran contrary to all commonsense, battled with fear, and on occasions lost.

Courage and faith go hand in hand. But courage does not mean an absence of fear. Courage is the ability to face fears head-on, and to go on in spite of them. Abraham, in this situation, had taken his eyes off God and begun to trust his very human feelings. Human logic told him to panic, but faith said stand still and trust God.

Fighting fear

My friend, the airline pilot who faced the bomb threat, told me about an old training trick. You sit in a swivel chair, arms folded, feet off the ground and eyes blindfolded. Someone spins the chair and the pilot sitting in it has to guess which way he is being turned and when he has stopped moving. The pilot never gets it right. The fluid in the ear canals distorts balance and perception.

The lesson for pilots is clear: there are times when your senses will tell you one thing and your instruments another. Believe the instruments. Pilots who have made the mistake of trusting themselves instead of their instruments rarely get the chance to try again.

As a Christian there will be occasions when everything in you says, 'Panic and run!' Part of growing up in God is learning when not to trust your own judgement, but to trust God.

Workout

1. Face fears head on! Do you know your own pet fears, and can you own up to them?

2. Share with a trusted friend (or friends) your fears and your desire to know God's help. ('Therefore confess your sins to each other and pray for each other so that you may be healed' James 5:16.)

3. Discover as many verses as possible in the Bible that deal with your particular fear. Memorize and meditate on them. (For example, Matthew 6:25–34; Romans 8:28–29; Philippians 4:13; Hebrews 12:1–13.)

4. When you feel overwhelmed by fear:

* Refuse to panic, and consciously trust God.

* Praise and worship the Lord, thanking him for who he is.

* Get another Christian to pray with you and for you.

5. When you know you have overcome fear in a particular situation, write it down. We so easily forget God's victories. Then pass it on—someone next to you may be struggling with the same fear!

Prayer

Dear Father, thank you that your love drives out my fear. Thank you for understanding me perfectly, for seeing me in my fear and for wanting to set me free. Please help me to face my fears, share them with you and others and then know your release from them. Thank you that I can read the words 'Do not fear' again and again in your word. Please help me to learn to trust you. Amen.

PS

For God did not give us a spirit of timidity—of cowardice, of craven and cringing and fawning fear—but He has given us a spirit of power and of love and of calm and well-balanced mind and discipline and self-control (2 Timothy 1:7, Amplified Version).

25

Loneliness

Reading

Psalm 25:1–22

Think through

The pips in the call box were going again and the money was fast running out. The machine was eating 10p pieces like they were going out of fashion, but this was an urgent call, money was no object.

A tearful Jackie was trying hard to explain to a distressed mother and father at the other end of the line why she wanted to quit university, pack her bags and catch the next train home. Mum and Dad were trying hard to understand. Jackie had seemed to settle in so well at the start of her first term. She'd made lots of friends, found a good local church to settle into and was actively involved in university life. But she'd picked up a bad case of mid-course blues and it had dragged on for weeks.

'I feel so lonely. I've got no one to talk to,' she explained.

'But what about your friends in the Christian Union?' asked Mum, trying to be helpful.

'I know,' replied Jackie, 'but they're all so busy and I just need someone that I can really trust before I can share how I feel.'

That real-life incident pinpoints one of the major problems some Christians face today: loneliness. Perhaps you can identify with Jackie's experience. Loneliness is exactly what it says—a sense of being cut off, completely alone. It is often accompanied by feelings of depression, fear and sometimes (if you're away from familiar surroundings) homesickness. It can even produce a physical ache.

You don't even have to be on a desert island to feel lonely. That's one of the strange things about it. You can be surrounded by people with lots of things to do, and yet still feel overwhelmed by loneliness. Starting at a new school or college, changing your job, moving house or going to a new church are all times when even the happiest people can experience the pain of loneliness. It is something that comes at different stages of our lives— ask some personal questions around your church and you'll soon discover that! Watching your friends get married and start families can produce an awful sense of being alone when you're single. Children starting school can affect a mum who is left with time on her hands. And people—even mature Christians—who lose their life-partner say that the hardest thing to come to terms with is the aching feeling of being alone.

I hope you are not too depressed by reading this! It's so good to realize that God understands our feelings. He made us and knows exactly how we work. One of the exciting things about being a Christian is discovering not only how God understands our needs but learning how he can meet them.

People in the Bible were no strangers to loneliness.

The greatest example of all is, of course, Jesus himself. When he said to the disciples, who kept nodding off in Gethsemane, 'My soul is overwhelmed with sorrow to the point of death. Stay here and keep watch with me' (Matthew 26:38), he was crying out for human company and fellowship in his hour of great need. Jesus knows about loneliness.

David experienced it too, and I am glad that he wrote about his feelings. Psalm 25:16–17 is a helpful prescription for lonely people. He spells out his feelings:

> Turn to me and be gracious to me,
>   for I am lonely and afflicted.
> The troubles of my heart have multiplied;
>   free me from my anguish.

We are not exactly certain when David wrote this Psalm, but it is obvious that he feels there are people who are against him. He had a turbulent life and it's obvious that he felt vulnerable at this particular time. But the important thing for us to notice is how he handled the problem of loneliness. We can see from this Psalm some of the positive steps that he took:

He looked to God (verses 1–2)

Why is it that when we are in trouble the one place we know we can find help is the last place we turn to?

He affirmed his faith (verses 8–10)

He reminds himself that God is good, upright, loving, faithful, forgiving and that he guides and teaches those who are truly open to him.

He recognized his need (verses 7, 11)

Whenever we draw near to God we are made aware of our sinfulness as compared to his utter holiness. I believe

David is aware that in some measure he is the author of his own problems. Getting close to God helps us to get a right perspective on ourselves.

He asked for help (verses 17–18, 20)

David was specific in what he asked God to do in this situation. He was anxious to learn God's ways even in the difficult times (see also Psalm 25:4–5).

He prayed for others (verse 22)

'Redeem Israel, O God!' seems a strange prayer in the middle of a long list of his own problems. But honest prayer has that sort of effect upon us. We get our eyes off ourselves on to God who, in turn, helps us to see others' needs as well as our own.

Now just in case you think I am saying that the only answer to loneliness is to 'go away and pray about it', stop and think for a moment. God gives us guidelines to live by—sensible rules that make for healthy living. David learned that, and, if we are willing, we can learn from his experience of how to handle a lonely heart.

The Beatles' classic song *Eleanor Rigby* has these haunting lyrics: 'All the lonely people, where do they all come from? All the lonely people, where do they all belong?' I find it helpful in my lonely moments to open my eyes and look around. Loneliness is a negative force, but we can turn it into a positive influence. God can use it to stir us up to action; to reach out and share the love of Jesus with people who are far lonelier than we are.

Imagine life without Jesus—no hope for today, or tomorrow. And if you have got good news to share, don't just sit there, say something!

By the way, my friend Jackie did sort things out. She took some positive steps to help herself and was honest enough to share with her Christian friends about her feelings. And through that experience I believe she has grown, and, hopefully, learned something very important about keeping her eyes open when she prays.

Workout

When you're feeling lonely...

1. Try and sort out your feelings. Is there a specific thing that you can pinpoint that produces feelings of being alone?

2. Are you committed to a fellowship of Christians where you can receive teaching, love and care?

3. Are there positive steps you can take to ease the problem of loneliness?

4. Have you shared your feelings with another Christian and asked for prayer and help?

5. Are there particular times when loneliness is more acute? What can you do to help yourself in such situations?

6. Have you asked God to show you people that you can actively get involved with and help?

7. One of the best ways to overcome lonely feelings is to reach out and share with someone else worse off than yourself; a coffee, a meal, or just a chat—all great antidotes to that lonely heart feeling...and it blesses someone else too!

Prayer

Father, I thank you that you have shared *all* my feelings. Jesus knew the desperation of being alone. Please help me to take the positive steps I can. Please don't let me get trapped into cutting myself off from others around me because I feel they're not interested and because I

feel on my own. Please help me to be willing to make the
first move and realize that I'm not alone! Amen.

PS

O Lord, you have searched me
  and you know me.
You know when I sit and when I rise;
  you perceive my thoughts from afar.
You discern my going out and my lying
    down;
  you are familiar with all my ways.
Before a word is on my tongue
  you know it completely, O Lord.
You hem me in, behind and before;
  you have laid your hand upon me.
Such knowledge is too wonderful for
    me,
  too lofty for me to attain.
Where can I go from your Spirit?
  Where can I flee from your presence?
If I go up to the heavens, you are there;
  if I make my bed in the depths, you
    are there.
If I rise on the wings of the dawn,
  if I settle on the far side of the sea,
even there your hand will guide me,
  your right hand will hold me fast.
If I say, 'Surely the darkness will hide
    me
  and the light become night around me,'
even the darkness will not be dark to
    you;
  the night will shine like the day,
  for darkness is as light to you.
                    (Psalm 139:1–12)

SECTION 6

James—
Act It Out

26

Tough Times

Readings

James 1:1–18; 5:7–11

Think through

It was obvious that the driver was tense as he swung his car into the side of the road. The street was packed—people walking, talking and laughing. Shop windows were brightly lit, even if sparsely furnished. It all looked normal. But living in that country is anything but normal, especially if you are a Christian.

My friend had been talking on the journey about the prospect of prison. He had lived with that possibility for years and even in front of his wife and young family the matter was discussed as routinely as a trip to the dentist. Not that he felt no fear. He freely talked about his anxieties, especially as Christians in prison could expect a rough ride. This small family had come to accept the awful possibility that a knock on the door could result in years of separation—even death.

I suppose that is what makes saying goodbye to a friend in those circumstances all the more special. We embraced; I stepped out of the car on to the crowded pavement and turned back to look at him.

'Pray for us,' were his last words as he smiled farewell and drove off into the night.

He is not alone. As I sit at my desk to write I have just looked up at my noticeboard and seen the photos of thirty-six men and women of all ages who are in prisons or labour camps because where they live their commitment to Jesus is out of step with 'good citizenship'. Thirty-six faces—somebody's husband, wife, son or daughter—and *my* brothers and sisters.

James wrote his practical letter to Christians who were facing tough times. And it is worth being reminded that just as it cost a lot to be a follower of Jesus in the first century, the price remains the same for many believers in a world 2,000 years down the road.

He begins his letter with what at first sounds like a strange piece of advice: 'Consider it pure joy, my brothers, whenever you face trials of many kinds' (James 1:2). How can any normal human being stay happy when everything is falling apart? Isn't this just another example of the Christian sado-masochism which produced the philosophy: 'If it's fun, it can't be spiritual!'? You need to read on to get the message straight.

The pressures we face

By 'trials of many kinds', James is referring to all the different types of pressures we face:

Pressures from outside

These include persecution, life's hard knocks and things that just go wrong.

Pressures from inside

This category would cover temptation and the powerful

pull of the old nature to go back to the old way of living.

James is saying that the way to cope with pressures—whether from without or within—is to respond with an attitude of 'pure joy', and he goes on to back up his case with some powerful reasons.

When the heat is on

In case we mistakenly think that God's message to people under pressure is simply, 'Grin and bear it!', James gives us the true perspective:

Testing produces stamina

'The testing of your faith develops perseverance' (James 1:3). The more you learn to handle pressure the more your spiritual stamina increases.

Like the lonely runner plodding the streets, only sustained training can build you up for a marathon. One reason to be joyful when the pressures come is that God is actually answering your prayers. His training plan is aimed towards one thing—'that you may be mature and complete, not lacking anything' (James 1:4).

Ask for wisdom

'If in doubt—shout!' is what James is getting at when he writes, 'If any of you lacks wisdom he should ask God' (James 1:5). How often do we do that when the heat is on? It is much more natural to moan or get angry with God, but we are told that he does not withhold wisdom from those who ask in faith. That doesn't mean we will always get an answer to the question 'Why?'. I simply don't know *why* some temptations won't stay dead or *why* a particular problem has arisen. But God has promised wisdom and two of the blessings of wisdom are a quiet heart and a peaceful mind.

Purpose in pain

There is no such thing as pointless suffering in the Christian life. James reminds us that a special blessing belongs to those who keep going under pressure. We are in a race, sitting an exam, facing a test. It has a limited span and, at the end, a prize worth waiting for (James 1:12).

How temptation works

God isn't the creator of temptation—it comes from our own sinful human nature and our magnetic attraction to things that are wrong.

James believes it is important that we know how temptation works (James 1:13–15). God is not causing that temptation to pull, but when it does occur he can use it. Even the toughest times can be turned around by God for our good and his glory (Romans 8:28).

Hang in there

Patience is something we all need. As James points out, the only way to a bumper harvest is to learn to wait patiently for the right amount of rain (James 5:7–11). We have plenty of examples in Scripture of those who kept going when everything told them to give in. Perhaps we need to pray more for patience and less for the pressure to go away?

God cares!

'The Lord is full of compassion and mercy' (James 5:11). This is a reminder we all need. In giving us practical ways to understand and cope with pressure, James doesn't want us to forget that God is not the celestial sadist some make him out to be. His whole nature is compassion and mercy. He cares! And that means he will not prolong the pressure any longer than is needed.

We had a break-in last night and something fairly special was stolen. I have spent most of the morning feeling angry and violated—wanting to find whoever did it and make them pay. J. B. Phillips translates James' advice:

> When all kinds of trials and temptations crowd into your lives, my brothers, don't resent them as intruders, but welcome them as friends (James 1:2).

There are two responses to pressures: resent them as unwanted intruders or welcome them as friends. With our burglary happening just a few hours ago that Scripture is painful. But there is a deep lesson that needs re-learning. Instead of seeing those familiar problems as obstacles we need to start treating them as opportunities.

Workout

1. What kind of pressures do you face? Are those pressures from outside or inside?

2. As we've read, God can use the negative things in our lives—the problems, difficulties and pressures—and bring something very positive out of them. Are you prepared to ask God to teach you something through them?

3. It's so easy to get wrapped up in our own problems and pressures. Ask God to open your eyes to see people around you who are really under pressure. It doesn't hurt to look further afield either and remember those people living in countries where they are persecuted for their faith. Pray for them.

Prayer

Father, it's hard to 'consider it pure joy' when I think of the pressures that are on me and the problems that I face. Father, please help me to learn to see those things as opportunities rather than obstacles in my Christian life. Thank you that you will never leave me and will provide the strength and resources I need to meet *every* situation in my life. Hallelujah! Amen.

PS

Therefore, since we have been justified through faith, we have peace with God through our Lord Jesus Christ, through whom we have gained access by faith into this grace in which we now stand. And we rejoice in the hope of the glory of God. Not only so, but we also rejoice in our sufferings, because we know that suffering produces perseverance; perseverance, character; and character, hope. And hope does not disappoint us, because God has poured out his love into our hearts by the Holy Spirit, whom he has given us (Romans 5:1–5).

27

Learning to Look

Readings

James 1:9–11; 2:1–13

Think through

I was once given a piece of advice which I have never forgotten: 'If you want to know a person's true character—look at how they treat someone who can't do anything for them.'

We are all guilty at times of using people for our own ends and the letter of James—practical as always—provides some useful teaching on learning to treat people the right way.

Take a practical example: every church, house group or young people's group contains the usual mixture of personality types we find in any social grouping. Alongside the extrovert characters there are the quieter more reflective types. And most groups will have the misfits who are sadly overlooked—or, worse still, avoided altogether. We have our code names for them, even if we are so spiritual we wouldn't dream of saying them out loud. We still pigeon-hole people like that in our hearts.

It is worth remembering that Jesus had a fair collection of social misfits around him who didn't exactly qualify for the Most Beautiful Person in Palestine Award. And the first Christian fellowships seem to have had their fair share of the uninfluential, as Paul points out:

> Brothers, think of what you were when you were called. Not many of you were wise by human standards; not many were influential; not many were of noble birth (1 Corinthians 1:26).

I have been struggling to write this during a busy overseas trip, where I've been visiting one of the front lines of Christian mission in today's world. Just a few nights ago I spent some time praying with a couple of lads in their twenties who are putting a lot on the line for their faith in Jesus. Quite literally they are taking enormous risks to bring the gospel to a group of unreached people. In your average British church they would be ignored. They would not fit comfortably into an average young people's group. Socially, materially and intellectually they could be overlooked, but spiritually—where it really counts—they are dynamite.

As we prayed together, the letter of James came alive to me in a new way. I realized that I too was guilty of putting people into categories and failing to see them from God's perspective. James gives us two important warnings in this area—the first about how we look at ourselves, and the second about how we look at others.

Looking at ourselves

Some people suffer from what is called an inferiority complex. They believe that because of their background or lack of education they don't have much to offer. Then there are people with the opposite problem—a superiority complex. They believe they are much better than others.

James writes some wise words about wrong attitudes towards ourselves:

To those who feel inferior:

'The brother in humble circumstances ought to take pride in his high position' (James 1:9). When we are tempted to self-pity and to count up a list of reasons why we don't fit the success pattern, the Bible reminds us of what we are, what we are becoming and, one day, what we shall be—all because of Jesus Christ (see 1 Corinthians 6:11; Colossians 1:27; 1 Peter 2:8–9).

To those who feel superior:

'But the one who is rich should take pride in his low position, because he will pass away like a wild flower' (James 1:10). Money, status and possessions are nothing in the light of eternity. James is reminding those who have the tendency to be proud about material things to boast instead about how the grace of God has reached them in their total need (see Matthew 5:3; 1 Timothy 6:17–19).

I remember once visiting a lighthouse and seeing the intricate way in which the light was set. The keeper pointed out the great accuracy with which the light was placed in relation to the giant reflectors. If it was too low, or on the other hand too high, the light was unable to achieve maximum range. In order to be seen from miles out at sea the setting had to be perfect.

In the same way, it is possible to have too high or too low an image of ourselves which cuts down the effectiveness of our lives for God.

Looking at others

Favouritism was obviously a problem in some of the churches James was writing to. It still is today. But the word of God makes no compromises: 'Don't show favouritism' (James 2:1).

Are we guilty of discriminating and judging people by the clothes they wear or their apparent lack of style? Do we judge people more by the High Street window than the content of their character? Are we guilty of writing someone off because their taste in music is weird or their accent strange?

James makes a point that a good deal of us ignore:

> If you really keep the royal law found in Scripture, 'Love your neighbour as yourself,' you are doing right. But if you show favouritism you sin and are convicted by the law as lawbreakers (James 2:8).

Showing favouritism means giving someone special attention at the expense of another person. Why not take an honest look around church this Sunday and see how well you are doing in the equality stakes?

Attitudes always govern actions. What we think, is seen in the way we behave. James later writes about the in-fighting among Christians that stems from jealousy (James 4:1–3) and against the terrible slanging matches that have ruined all too many churches (James 4:11–12). That is why he hits at the root of the problem by urging God's people to honestly examine their heart attitudes towards others.

We rightly react when a person is mistreated because of the colour of his skin, but prejudices are not always to do with racial divisions. Churches and youth groups can be divided along other lines, such as old versus young, charismatic versus non-charismatic, singles versus marrieds. Prejudice rears its ugly head too whenever we make a distinction in our minds between the in-crowd and the outcasts. Try watching your own attitudes next time you're in a room where there are those you like to be liked by and those you usually overlook.

Some of God's best gifts come in strange-looking parcels. By building a bridge of friendship to someone who can't do anything for you, you may just be opening up your life to a special blessing that you never expected.

Workout

1. How true a picture do we have of ourselves? We've been reminded that both a sense of inferiority and a sense of superiority are wrong. We can know that God values us as we are, but also that he knows our faults and failings. ('He loves us just as we are, but loves us too much to leave us as we are.')

2. It is virtually impossible to look at everybody in an unbiased way. We all make certain judgements about people and have our own standards that we expect them to live up to. How do you judge another person? How do you gain a first impression of somebody?

3. Be honest enough to take a look around church this Sunday. Recognize the way in which you make judgements and show favouritism. Ask God's forgiveness and then try to reach out to someone you've rejected in the past.

Prayer

Father, please forgive me that even as I've read this chapter I've been trying to make excuses—telling myself that it doesn't apply to me because I accept everyone. Father, thank you for reminding me of the people I *don't* talk to when I walk into church. Thank you that you have accepted me and for helping me to see that that gives me every reason to accept each one of my brothers and sisters. Thank you, Father. Amen.

PS

There is only one Lawgiver and Judge, the one who is able to save and destroy. But you—who are you to judge your neighbour (James 4:12)?

28

Hearing and Doing

Readings

James 1:22–27; 2:14–17; 3:13–18

Think through

It might be good for the state of Britain if all church services carried a compulsory 'Spiritual Health Warning'. Imagine the Church Bulletin next Sunday bearing the red-boxed message: 'WARNING: Attendance at this service may seriously affect your spiritual health.'

Possibly congregations would diminish—but at least we'd be moving towards a more radical understanding of biblical Christianity. In his open letter to Christians, James issues a spiritual health warning about the danger of hearing the word of God and doing nothing about it. He would have some sympathy with G. K. Chesterton who wrote: 'The Christian ideal has not been tried and found wanting. It has been found difficult—and left untried.'

James is concerned that Christians get their act

together and start to practise what they claim to believe. He pinpoints some areas for action:

Hearing God's word

'Do not merely listen to the word, and so deceive yourselves. Do what it says' (James 1:22). That is a direct warning about hearing God's truth and remaining totally unchanged by it.

I remember once visiting a beautiful old English parish church. Walking along the path after the service I spotted some words carved into the wooden beam above the lych-gate: 'Blessed rather are those who hear the word of God and obey it.' (The words of Jesus from Luke 11:28.) What a reminder every time we leave church or come away from reading the Bible. It is one thing to hear, but do we obey?

Look into it

Reading the Bible and failing to obey the message is like looking into a mirror then going away and forgetting what you look like (James 1:23–24). We all know about frantic dashes first thing in the morning. That time when —still semi-conscious—we attempt to do six things simultaneously, all the time hoping that the clock is a few minutes fast. A quick look in the mirror to rearrange those bits that are still rearrangable and we rush off to face the world for another day. But unless we're going for an interview, meeting a special person or we've just heard the latest 'Love Yourself' ministry tape from the USA, we don't study what we look like.

The same mad rush can apply to our attitude to God. A quick glance at the Bible and a few disjointed prayers are not the best way to build a solid relationship. In our high-pressure world we need to learn how to stop, and give God space.

James spells out what's involved: 'The man who looks intently into the perfect law . . . will be blessed in what he does' (James 1:25). The word translated as 'looks intently' means to 'peer into'. It is the same word used of Peter and Mary when they bent over and looked into the empty tomb (John 20:5, 11). God's word brings freedom when we look into it like that and apply it to our lives.

Obey it

'Do what it says' (James 1:22) is James' stark instruction. How much of the teaching that we hear do we actually put into practice? Often we can learn from how others see us—even if the criticism stings a little. Try this for size from the pen of Thomas Russell Ybarra: 'A Christian is a man who feels repentance on a Sunday for what he did on Saturday and is going to do on Monday.'

Charles Swindoll tells a disturbing parable in one of his books about the boss of a large corporation who leaves his manager in charge while he goes abroad on a long business trip. The boss keeps in touch regularly and sends telex messages with precise instructions on how the company is to run in his absence. He returns to find everything in chaos. When he asks why his instructions have not been carried out, he is told how his enthusiastic employees had received all his telexes and preserved them carefully in the files. The extra-keen members had even memorized whole chunks of his detailed instructions and could recite them to order. They had also arranged study seminars to examine in great detail the exact meaning of various words that were used in the instructions. One vital ingredient was missing—no one had actually done what they were told to do.

Ouch! The story makes a painful point. God prizes obedience far more than expertise in textual criticism. We may be great shakes on the interpretation of the tent-pegs in the Tabernacle, but if we can't control our temper then we have a long way to go in spiritual maturity.

Doing God's will

The letter of James is so intensely practical it is downright uncomfortable. He seems intent to earth the truth of what he is saying in everyday examples of Christian living.

True spirituality

How well do we control our tongues (James 1:26)? How is our faith expressed in terms of caring for people with deep needs (James 1:27; 2:14–17)? These are the marks of true spirituality.

True wisdom

This is seen in a pure life which is peace-loving, considerate towards others, submissive in tough situations, full of mercy and kindness. It is recognized in those who are impartial in their judgements of others and have sincere hearts after God. These are the sort of people who are peacemakers determined to build bridges for God—concerned to draw others in rather than cut them off (James 3:17–18).

Doing God's will always involves practically working it out in everyday living. Poor old James has had a rough press over the years. Martin Luther did him no great favour when he wrote his famous assessment of the letter: 'Therefore is St James' Epistle a right strawy epistle...for it has no gospel character to it.' That has got to rank alongside the studio report on Fred Astaire's first screen test as one of the most ill-judged statements of all time. Some anonymous studio employee recorded, of Astaire, 'Can't act, can't sing. Slightly bald. Can dance a little.'

The Epistle of James is packed with gospel-character and deserves to be rescued from the back corner of the Christian library shelves. He is concerned with Christian action. And in a world so often unmoved by our multiplicity of words we badly need some of that. It all starts with listening, looking…then doing.

Workout

1. When you read the Bible or hear a sermon do you ask God to speak to you? Do you also ask him what he wants you to do in response to that word?

2. True spirituality isn't having your head in the clouds so much as having your feet on the ground! We so often stress personal piety as a negative force stopping us getting involved, but our relationship with God should lead to action—as we show his love and compassion in a hurting world. How spiritual are you?

3. True wisdom isn't pronouncing judgements on everyone except ourselves! 'But the wisdom that comes from heaven is first of all pure; then peace-loving, considerate, submissive, full of mercy and good fruit, impartial and sincere' (James 3:17). How wise are you?

Prayer

Dear Father, thank you that we have so many opportunities to hear your word, so many versions of the Bible and numerous Christian books to read. Forgive us, that despite all this, we tend to take your word for granted. Father, please make your word come alive to me. Give me new insights and, by the power of your holy Spirit in me, help me to obey your word and really live out what I believe. Amen.

PS

Psalm 119:105–106 in the Living Bible shows something of God's word—something that leads us and guides us *as we go*. It's not only for lighting the spot where we are now . . . but for helping us to move ahead:

Your words are a flashlight to light the path ahead of me, and keep me from stumbling. I've said it once and I'll say it again and again: I will obey these wonderful laws of yours.

29

Tame that Tongue!

Reading

James 3:1–12

Think through

An American newspaper recently unveiled the latest
time-saving device for high-pressured people: an on-
board computer that will run your bath as you drive
home from the office. You can step right from the car
into the tub, saving yet more minutes in your busy
schedule.

I wish someone would come up with a device for
humans like the replay facility on cassette recorders. If
only we could record over some of the things we wish
we'd never said and lose for ever the memory of words
which have caused so much damage.

James gives some helpful teaching on taming the
tongue. He mentions it in the same breath as warning
teachers of the word that they will be strictly judged. It is
a solemn reminder that anyone who teaches needs to be
seeking to live out the truth that they teach (James 3:1).
He then adds a word of encouragement to teachers and

preachers: 'We all stumble in many ways' (James 3:2). No one has reached perfection, and to illustrate he points to the most dangerous part of our bodies—the tongue.

The power of the tongue

James paints six vivid pictures which teach us about the power of the tongue:

Horses (James 3:3)

A small bit in the mouth of a horse controls the movement of a mighty animal. Compared with the size of the horse it controls, the bit is tiny, but its power is awesome. The tongue is like that. Don't underestimate its ability to control you.

Ships (James 3:4)

A large sailing ship is driven by strong winds, but it is the rudder—again, small in comparison—which sets its direction. Our tongues direct our lives in the same way.

Forest fires (James 3:5)

We have all seen films of forests ablaze. Destruction and death on a massive scale are caused by a small spark. How many times in human history has irreparable damage been caused by destructive words that have been carelessly discarded like a cigarette end?

The animal world (James 3:7)

Mankind has learned to tame animals, birds, reptiles and fish, but 'no man can tame the tongue'. We may have power to train dolphins to do aerobics, fleas to jump through hoops and lions to act like pussy cats—but without the power of God's Spirit we can't control our tongues.

Water springs (James 3:11)

Whoever heard of a spring that delivered fresh water and salt water at the same time? That is the same ridiculous inconsistency as a person who sings 'Jesus we enthrone you' at the top of his voice and twenty minutes later is passing on some juicy piece of gossip about someone in the house group. Out of the same mouth we praise God and curse man.

Fig trees and grapevines (James 3:12)

Can you imagine a fig tree that produced olives or a grapevine that gave figs! You can tell the nature of the tree by the fruit it produces. Jesus said, 'Out of the overflow of the heart the mouth speaks' (Matthew 12:34). If you want a true assessment of how you are growing in God, try listening to your own conversation for a day. Words are a mirror of the soul.

In case you haven't got the point, James reminds us of the source of the tongue's destructive power:

> The tongue also is a fire, a world of evil among the parts of the body. It corrupts the whole person, sets the whole course of his life on fire, and is itself set on fire by hell (James 3:6).

The control of the tongue

Marriages are broken, friendships ruined, churches split, characters assassinated. From punch-ups in the playground to wars between nations, the uncontrolled tongue has caused untold havoc.

Short of taking a Trappist vow of silence, what can be done to master the mouth?

Guard your heart

Jesus said that the mouth is the heart's overflow; it reveals what we are truly like. The wise words of Proverbs remind us: 'Above all else, guard your heart, for it is the well-spring of life' (Proverbs 4:23). The heart is the soil in which the fruit of the Spirit takes root. Hearts easily become overgrown with weeds; become hard and unresponsive to the voice of God. That is why the heavenly Gardener needs to have constant access to our hearts to carry out the regular spade work we all require.

Renew your mind

We are told that the key to a transformed life is a renewed mind (Romans 12:2). In practical terms that means a stock-take of our personal weaknesses. Am I jealous? Then I need the Holy Spirit to teach me about an attitude of love. Am I critical? Then I must train my mind to see the good in people. Am I quick to lose my temper? Then I need the Spirit's fruit of patience. Try a three-times-a-day dose of Philippians 4:8,

> Whatever is true, whatever is noble, whatever is right, whatever is pure, whatever is lovely, whatever is admirable —if anything is excellent or praiseworthy—think about such things.

Watch your mouth

The tongue can hurt—'it is a restless evil, full of deadly poison' (James 3:8)—but by the power of God's redeeming love it can heal. Part of spiritual discipline is learning how to harness the power of the tongue. We can worship and praise God with the tongue. We can also help people. We need to learn how to heal, encourage, inspire, build up, teach, exhort and bless. It is amazing to see how a God-controlled tongue can repair what it had previously ripped apart.

I can only have been fourteen when, during a family holiday, I took an early morning walk along a cliff top. He was an elderly man with no great gift of eloquence but a genuine concern for a teenage rebel. I wasn't a Christian and showed no interest in becoming one, but it didn't stop me noticing godliness. 'Think of the number of words you speak in a day,' he said. I did. It was an uncomfortable thought. He then let this young pagan in on a secret of his walk with God. A secret that lay forgotten for years. 'I always make sure that the first person I speak to every day of my life is Jesus. And I ask him to watch and control all the other words that I am going to speak that day.'

The elderly saint had a point. In a world bombarded with words it is worth remembering the wisdom of Proverbs 10:19, in the inimitable paraphrase of the Living Bible: 'Don't talk so much. Every time you open your mouth you put your foot in it. Be sensible and turn off the flow!'

Workout

1. Just think of how much you say each day. Is it all positive and helpful? As you go through a day, make a note of the positive and negative things that you say.

2. It's one thing to sort this out for ourselves, but another when we're with a group of friends with a track record of gossip and harmful conversation. Do you have the strength to stand against negative, back-biting talk? It will take a conscious decision and a real reliance on God's strength.

3. Look at the steps mentioned in controlling the tongue: guard your heart, renew your mind and watch

your mouth. What positive steps can you take to do those things, draw closer to God and become more like Jesus?

Prayer

Dear Father, you know that there are numerous occasions I can think of when I've said too much or said the wrong thing. As you remind me of those times I bring them to you and ask your forgiveness. Please draw me closer to yourself and help me to reject gossip and negative talk. You know how hard it's going to be for me to put that into practice. I ask for your strength and say again that I want you to make me more like Jesus. Amen.

PS

Your attitude should be the same as that of Christ Jesus... Do everything without complaining or arguing, so that you may become blameless and pure, children of God without fault in a crooked and depraved generation, in which you shine like stars in the universe as you hold out the word of life—in order that I may boast on the day of Christ that I did not run or labour for nothing (Philippians 2:5, 14–16).

30

Dead or Alive?

Reading

James 2:14–26

Think through

Being misunderstood is a rotten experience. I should know, it happened to me only yesterday when a telephone message was passed on wrongly and what was intended as a compliment had been interpreted as a criticism. It took some explaining to sort the muddled message out.

James' letter has drawn a lot of flak over the centuries. He has often been accused of dangerous teaching—if not downright heresy. But the accusations have come from those who haven't taken time to listen carefully to what is being said.

His letter is part of our Bible, and as such it is an important part of the 'God-breathed' (or inspired) word. This last look at some of the themes of the letter of James takes us across a minefield—so watch out! In chapter 2, verses 14–26, James draws attention to the strong link between faith and deeds. How does what a person believes affect the way he behaves?

James makes his case with some blunt language and his verbal hand-grenades have caused a few loud explosions. Some have felt he contradicts the Apostle Paul who, in his letters to the Romans and Galatians, emphasizes justification by faith—that is, how a person is made right with God through trusting in Jesus Christ, not by their own good works. But in his letter, James makes statements like: 'A person is justified by what he does and not by faith alone' (James 2:24). Is this yet another example of the many so-called contradictions in the Bible that critics frequently point to?

Those who have put Paul and James into opposite corners of the boxing ring have made an expensive mistake. They have only listened to part of the argument. Paul has no room for faith that has no love to back it up (see Romans 2:5–6; 13:12; Galatians 5:6, 13; Ephesians 2:10). Neither does James say anything out of line with the rest of the New Testament. In fact, he echoes the teaching of Jesus himself when he talked about men seeing our good deeds and praising God because of them (Matthew 5:16).

The 'fighters' are in fact friends—which only goes to show how careful we must be in listening to and weighing up arguments. Guard against that horrible part of human nature that likes to put people into opposite camps and create trouble where none exists. It breaks the heart of God, divides the body of Christ and quenches the Holy Spirit.

Root and fruit

God's grace (his undeserved kindness) is the *soil*. Faith is the *root* that goes deep into the soil to draw life and nourishment. Deeds are the *fruit* produced by lives that draw on the strength and power of God. Paul is writing

to young Christians and is concerned that their
understanding of God's grace is clear—he is
concentrating on their roots. James, on the other hand,
is dealing with believers who are in danger of forgetting
that their lives must produce the fruit of God's grace. He
makes a vital distinction between:

Dead faith (James 2:14–19)

Dead faith is easy to recognize. It is all in the mouth and
the mind. Spiritual words are easy to come by (there is
such a thing as 'Jesus jargon'). There is someone in your
church in desperate financial need and you wish them
well and promise to pray for them, but do nothing to
help—that is dead faith. Like the homeless woman who
turned to a vicar for help and received none. She wrote
this poem in her desperation and handed it to a regional
officer for Shelter—the campaign for the homeless.

I was hungry,
  and you formed a humanities group to discuss my hunger.
I was imprisoned,
  and you crept off quietly to your chapel and prayed for
  my release.
I was naked,
  and in your mind you debated the morality of my
  appearance.
I was sick,
  and you knelt and thanked God for your health.
I was homeless,
  and you preached to me of the spiritual shelter of
  the love of God.
I was lonely,
  and you left me alone to pray for me.
You seem so holy, so close to God,
  But I am still very hungry—and lonely—and cold.

Dead faith is all in the mind, it never travels further.
Even the demons have intellectual belief, but it doesn't

with a brochure full of hype, or one that for all its plain looks performs reliably and efficiently there really is no contest.

At the end of the day, it is not a glossy exterior and fine-sounding words that count, but getting the job done. In order to be salt and light in a decaying and darkening world you need to know the vital difference between faith that's dead and faith that's alive.

Workout

1. How is your life different now from the time before you became a Christian? Is it just that you've added a couple of extra activities to your life (for example, going to church, reading your Bible, etc)? Or has there been a change in your behaviour?

2. Does your faith show up in actions? Do people know you're a Christian, not simply because you go to church, but by the way you live? ('If you were arrested for being a Christian, would there be enough evidence to convict you?')

Prayer

Father, thank you for the life you have given me. Please forgive me that so often my walk with you is so personal that no one knows about it. Please forgive me that my faith is sometimes only characterized by words. Thank you for all you have shown me about being practical and real. Please help me to live each day for you and may my actions, as well as my words, express my love for you. Amen.

PS

Living faith doesn't ignore the mind—it should be
thought out. It doesn't bypass the mouth—it needs to be
spoken out. But living faith cannot neglect the will—it
must be lived out.

What Next?

Getting to grips with the Bible is one of the surest ways to grow as a follower of Jesus Christ. We trust that this book has helped you to gain a better understanding of the word of God and its application to your life.

Having worked through this book on your own or as part of a group you may be looking for similar material to help you explore the message of the Bible further. We have listed below a few groups that specialize in providing good quality Bible study materials. If you write to them enclosing a stamped addressed envelope, they will be able to send you a list of their current publications.

A visit to your local Christian bookshop would also help you to discover the literature best suiting your needs. Every month new materials are published and if you explain to a member of the bookshop staff what you are looking for they will be able to give up-to-date information.

Whatever you choose to do, the system is only a means to an end. God wants to meet us through the reading of his word. He wants to touch, change, direct and bless our lives. The Bible is one of his choicest gifts and we need to guard against taking it for granted. One of the surest ways to avoid this is to use what you study from the Bible to power your prayers. Studying the Bible can easily become a dull academic exercise. To make it a life-changing reality prayer must be included.

Andrew Murray was a wise Christian who enjoyed a deep relationship with God. He once wrote these words:

> Little of the Word with little prayer is death to the spiritual life.
> Much of the Word with little prayer gives a sickly life.
> Much prayer with little of the Word gives more life but without steadfastness.
> A full measure of the Word and prayer each day gives a healthy and powerful life....

Useful addresses

Scripture Union, 130 City Road, London EC1V 2NJ.

Scripture Union publish a wide range of daily Bible reading notes covering all ages and levels of Christian growth. They are a well established agency with years of experience in the field of relating the study of God's word to the contemporary world.

Crusade for World Revival, PO Box 11, Walton-on-Thames, Surrey KT12 1BD.

CWR publish the popular *Every Day with Jesus* Bible reading notes. They also have an excellent study course which takes you through the entire Bible in a year, as well as materials for new Christians, children and young people.

Inter-Varsity Press, 38 De Montfort Street, Leicester, LE1 7GP.

IVP's *Know Your Bible* is a series of workbooks

covering the whole Bible in just over two years, involving nine proven methods of effective study. In spite of their publisher's name, it is not just for university types!

The Bible Society, Stonehill Green, Westlea, Swindon, Wilts SN5 7DG.

They produce a variety of Bible study aids. Their group study publications have been widely acclaimed and used in churches and house groups of all denominations.

Scripture Press, Raans Road, Amersham-on-the-Hill, Bucks HP6 6JQ.

They have published a number of books to help Christians get to grips with the message of the Bible. The *Bible Knowledge Commentary* based on the New International Version gives a verse-by-verse analysis of the Bible in separate Old Testament and New Testament volumes.

Navpress, Tregaron House, 27 High Street, New Malden, Surrey KT3 4BY.

This is the publishing arm of The Navigators, a worldwide interdenominational group committed to evangelism and discipling new Christians. Thousands of Christians have been grounded in the basics of the faith through Navigator publications. Their group study material is first class.

Pennies for Heaven

by Ian Coffey

'God loves a cheerful giver' – but how do I become cheerful? Where does *giving* fit into my whole spiritual life as a disciple of Christ?

In Pennies for Heaven *Ian Coffey shows how our view of God will affect every area of our life, including our grip on temporal possessions. I highly recommend his biblical call to acknowlege God as the Lord of all our life – and to give accordingly.*

LUIS PALAU
International Evangelist

Ouch! So much more than a book about money. Prods a prophetic finger at the real issue of discipleship in today's church.

PETER MEADOWS
Publishing Director, Buzz and Family Magazines

It's time that we made a statement as evangelicals about a materialistic society. Not to condemn, but to show God's own radical alternative. We have compromised for too long! This book must be compulsory reading for all Christians, young and old, if we are to live in God's world God's way.

CLIVE CALVER
General Secretary, Evangelical Alliance

Ian Coffey is a trustee of Saltmine Trust, an organization committed to a worldwide ministry of teaching and evangelism. He is also an associate minister of Earl's Hall Baptist Church, Southend. He is married with three children.

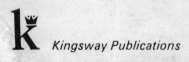

Kingsway Publications

change the way they act! William Barclay has pointed out that you can believe that the square on the hypotenuse of a right-angled triangle equals the sum of the square on the other two sides without it radically affecting the way you live today! 'Faith by itself, if it is not accompanied by action, is dead' (James 2:17).

Living faith (James 2:20–26)

Faith and deeds belong together and, in case he was thought to be going off the rails, James backs up his argument with two examples from the Old Testament: Abraham the patriarch and Rahab the prostitute.

Abraham (James 2:21–23) demonstrated that he trusted God when he was willing to sacrifice his son Isaac. Rahab (James 2:25) proved she was a believer when she risked her life to hide the two Israeli spies in her house. (For the whole story read Joshua 2:1–24.) In both cases their faith and their actions were working together.

Living faith doesn't ignore the mind—it should be thought out. It doesn't bypass the mouth—it needs to be spoken out. But living faith cannot neglect the will—it must be lived out.

Jesus Christ died to save all of us, so we must make sure we give him all there is of us so that we can live out a grateful life.

I had a fascinating chat with a salesman a few days ago as I was looking over an impressive display of new washing machines. Having listened to his patter I slipped him the question that I always use on such occasions: 'If you were buying one for yourself—which one would *you* choose?' Without hesitating he pointed at one in the corner which was positively dull in comparison with its gleaming rivals. 'It's not as flash as the rest,' the salesman admitted, 'but it does the best job of the lot.'

Faced with the choice of a flashy machine, backed up